MW00579298

THIS DEVOTIONAL BELONGS TO

_____

STOP THE SPIRAL

100 Days of
BREAKING FREE
from Negative Thoughts

DEVOTIONAL

JENNIE ALLEN

WATERBROOK

A NOTE FROM JENNIE

God has great timing. Perhaps you're seeing this in your life.

Many of us have experienced a bit of a wake-up call recently, whether due to global unrest, political tensions, or personal challenges. We've been forced to stop and look at the state of our minds. Or we've been confronted with changes that have happened inside us over weeks, months, and years, and we don't exactly like what we see. But if you've opened this book, maybe it's because you've sensed that now is the time to do something about all that is swirling in and around you.

For so many of us, who have been paddling busily on the lake of our lives, the lake has suddenly drained, and we've seen what was at the bottom. And what it was, was a lot of mess. A lot of turmoil and mental suffering. And rather than being new junk, maybe it's been on the bottom of our lakes for quite some time—ignored or shoved out of sight until now.

But gazing down at it, many of us are thinking, *Wow, I think I've been anxious for a long time, but I've been busy enough that I didn't notice.* Or, *Wow, I've felt depressed and tired for a long time, and maybe I need to get some help.* As we consider the state of our minds, we're realizing, something's got to change.

We need a new normal.

Maybe you've been struggling with low levels of anxiety for a long time. Or maybe you've recently experienced a season of difficulty or stress that has caused a spike of anxiety. The past few years of unrest and uncertainty have definitely revealed hidden anxieties many of us were already feeling. Whatever your unique situation, you might be asking, *What am I supposed to do with these thoughts? What do I do with these feelings?*

What if I told you that you don't have to spiral in toxic thoughts anymore? What if I told you that God has the power not only to save our souls but also to change our lives? I've seen Him do this for other people, and I have seen Him do this in me.

A few years ago, I went through a season of attack. It was quiet, it was subtle, and I barely noticed, honestly. It came every night at 3 a.m., when I was jolted awake, and simmering anxieties and doubts began to fill my mind. It beat me up for month upon month. And the bad part was, I didn't even realize it was happening. I thought it was just inevitable, that I had no control over it. I was at war with the devil in the night, but I never admitted it out loud. For eighteen months I never told anybody what was happening. When I finally did mention it to people, the second I did, it was obvious: *This was not who I was.* I had been spiraling down, listening to lies. But I didn't see it because I was not guarding my mind.

So what happened during month after month of me waking up in the middle of the night, and hearing the devil telling me whatever the heck he wanted alone in the dark? There was a cost to my faith. And to my health. And to my relationships. Patterns of toxic thinking became grooved into my mind. Maybe you know what that's like—that suffering and feeling out of control. But I can also tell you, when I realized I could fight it, everything shifted.

I believe we are at war and that the enemy of our souls is coming for us in ways that we hardly notice: in the fears and anxieties in our minds. I believe that for you, in some way, the enemy is targeting the peace of your mind. Those lies are real to you and coming at you every day.

In our generation, we're facing some unique spirals that pull us down and rob us of peace and joy and of the effectiveness that we could have for the kingdom of God. In this journey of rewiring downward spirals, we'll approach them one by one. We'll also look at research in psychology and neuroscience, because in studies of the brain, you cannot deny the power of God in the ways He built our minds. When it comes to the science of the brain, it backs up the Bible. It's wild. All the truths the Bible gives us about our minds—that we can take every thought captive and that we have power over our thoughts—all of these truths are spelled out in science. It's true. There's hope. We can change our minds.

Consider this one-hundred-day devotional your invitation to start noticing spiraling thought patterns—every day. To start getting wise to these toxic thought spirals that have taken so much of your life and peace. Yes, the enemy is targeting you. But I am here to tell you, God loves you, and He is also fighting for you. Our God says that we have the power to destroy strongholds. That we can be transformed by the renewal of our minds, which direct how we will live, who we will love, and what we will do with our time on this earth.

Breaking the cycle of toxic thoughts is an active process, which is why it's important to take it day by day—not passively thinking about whatever pops into our heads, but actively fighting to believe truth and to fix our eyes on Jesus, the author and perfecter of our faith. As we fixate on Him, the things of this earth grow less powerful. This is how we change. Imperfectly, slowly, messily even, but turning to Jesus again and again. Jesus is so real and present and here for us in this process, even as we fall and get back up.

What's on the other side of this fight? Now that I have done war with this part of my life, after going through it myself, I've never been more joyful, I've never been more free, I've never been more grateful, and I've never been more peaceful.

Of course I still spiral sometimes. Life on this earth can never be an endless victory lap. The goal, though, is not to be some kind of perfect mental ninja. It's to come closer to the God who adores us, who made our minds, and who made it possible for us to join Him in walking in the freedom He gives. Because God has grace for me and you, and wants our freedom, we can want it for ourselves. And because it's not done in my own strength or your own strength, we can breathe and have hope that God will do the freeing as we turn to Him each day.

A lot can happen in one hundred days. Mental pathways can be rewritten. Minds can be freed. Spirals can be flipped upside down.

Whether you go into this journey on your own with a journal and your Bible or with friends and partners fighting for each other, take this time to get honest and to think about your thoughts. To go to war against lies. To expand your understanding and compassion. To connect. To pray. To renew your reliance on a God who sets you free.

In this book, you'll find one hundred days of devotions to challenge your thinking, to encourage you, and to remind you of God's sufficiency and grace on the road to rewiring negative spirals. Each day's reading includes the following:

- *a short devotional essay*
- *verses for meditating on and soaking your soul in God's Word*
- *a "Rewire the Spiral" statement to speak over yourself*
- *a prayer for sparking a daily conversation with the Creator of your soul, who wants to bring peace to your mind*

I believe that the battle for your mind matters more than we can understand, and that God wants you to live more freely than you are right now. So I am praying huge prayers for you. But I also want to pray small prayers—that you'll see a glimmer of hope, that God will set you free, and that you will have your eyes opened. That you will see in a new way the enemy and what he wants for you, and that you will have nothing to do with it. That you would go to war. That you would fight better than you ever have, and that you would know what it is to rewire the spirals in your mind, in Jesus's name.

BEFORE YOU BEGIN

YOUR MENTAL HEALTH

You may have lived with low-grade sadness for as long as you can remember. Or maybe for you, it's far worse than that—a daily struggle, accompanied even by suicidal thoughts.

If mental illness is a struggle you face, may I please wrap loving arms around you, look you in the eyes, and whisper, "This—your anxiety or depression or bipolar disorder or suicidal thoughts—is not your fault"?

You may be suffering from a true chemical breakdown in your body. I get that. Several members of my family depend on medicine to help regulate their brain chemistry. Please hear me: There is no shame in that choice. Praise God for tools that help.

I just want you to know—please, lean in close and hear this—that throughout this book, whenever I talk about God giving us a choice about how we think, I am not suggesting that you can think your way out of mental illness. I am not. I have experienced seasons of anxiety so brutal that I was paralyzed.

There are seasons when we need help in the form of counseling and medicine. But I hope to show you in the coming pages that in every season there is help we can access for ourselves. And that learning to think a single thought can help each one of us—those of us who struggle with mental illness and those whose struggles are of a different sort.

THE STARTING LINE

I can't imagine a more anxious and spiraling feeling than being unsure about the meaning of life and the future of my soul. So before we begin, I would like to share the foundational truth that shapes the entire perspective of this devotional: We have been created on purpose for a purpose. We are designed for an intimate relationship with God forever. That is the context in which we begin to stop our spirals, to get out of our heads, and to be truly free in our souls and minds. Saint Augustine said, "You have made us for Yourself, and our hearts are restless until they find their rest in You."[1] In other words, we will forever spin out until we know the One who saves us.

So if you are unsure today if you know Jesus, or if you need reminding of what He has done to make your healing possible, here's the foundation for everything we're going to talk about in these one hundred days: the gospel, or the good news.[2]

---

1   Augustine of Hippo, *Saint Augustine's Confessions*, trans. Albert C. Outler (Mineola, NY: Courier Dover, 2002), 103.
2   Adapted from Jennie Allen, *Made for This* (Nashville: W Publishing, 2019), 269–70.

We had a perfect relationship with God until sin entered the world through Adam and Eve. And with sin came the promise of death and eternal separation from God. But from the moment of the first sin, God issued a promise that would bring us back to Him.

The penalty had to be paid.

Our sin was to be placed on a perfect sacrifice. God would send His own blameless, perfect Son to bear our sin and suffer our fate—to get us back.

Jesus came fulfilling thousands of years of prophecy, lived a perfect life, and died a gruesome death, reconciling our payment for our sin. Then after three days, He defeated death, rose from the grave, and now is seated with the Father, waiting for us.

Anyone who accepts the blood of Jesus for the forgiveness of their sin is adopted as a child of God and is issued God's very own Spirit, who seals and empowers us to live this life for Him.

Our souls will spin, restless and wanting, until they rest in God. After all, we were made for Him, and He gave everything so that our souls could finally and forever rest in Him.

If you have never trusted Christ for the forgiveness of your sins, you can trust Him this moment. Just tell Him your need for Him and tell Him of your trust in Him as your Lord and Savior. That's where everything begins.

EMOTION

THOUGHT

BEHAVIOR

RELATIONSHIPS

CONSEQUENCE

INTRODUCING
THE
SPIRAL

YOU ARE NOT A PROJECT TO BE FIXED

WHEN I FIRST STARTED TO THINK ABOUT MY THOUGHTS, I VIEWED MY mind as something I could fix. But the longer I thought about it, the more I realized that my mind is part of me, and it does the things it does to attempt to take care of me. There are *reasons* I struggle with doubt and fear and anxiety and anger. Good reasons. And for you, I know it's true too. If we never go back and really look compassionately at why we get where we are in our spirals, we end up with the shame of having to "fix it." And we end up with more shame when it breaks again.

But God is a God of mercy. We see that throughout the entire Bible.

In the Old Testament, He is patient with Israel and continues to give chance after chance. He is patient with David and the mistakes David makes, calling him a man after His own heart even when David does unthinkable things that we all would write him off, cancel him, and push him away for. He loves David throughout the span of his life, not just when he is winning but when he's confessing appalling sins.

In the New Testament, we see a compassionate God in Jesus. We see a God who came to earth to rescue people from their own decisions. We see a God who said, *You know what? I will make a way for all the places where you have messed up. I won't even ask you to fix it. I will fix it.*

The story of Jesus is not one in which we got our act together and then God saved us. It's one in which we were completely dead in our transgressions and in our mistakes, and God rescued us anyway and set us apart.

The whole of the Bible is super clear on the fact that we have limits, that we're going to make mistakes, that we are not completely curable on earth, and yet that we're filled with the Spirit who is helping us. We are new creations that can produce good and the fruit of the Spirit. And yet we're still going to struggle with our flesh and with our minds, daily.

I'd never want you to think that you're easily fixable. Or that on the days when you spiral, you should feel shame in any way. If anything, you should feel hope that you need God, and that we have a God who is accessible to us when we come to Him. He has compassion for us, so we can have compassion for ourselves.

MEDITATE:
God, being rich in mercy, because of the great love with which he loved us, even when we were dead in our trespasses, made us alive together with Christ—by grace you have been saved. (Ephesians 2:4–5)

REWIRE THE SPIRAL:
I do not have to fix myself because Jesus died to make me right with God.

God, thank You for being a God of mercy. When I get tired on this journey, when I hit my limits, wash me again in Your patience, Your love, Your compassion. Amen.

HOW QUIETNESS BREAKS OUR SPIRALS

OF ALL THE HARD WORK WE DO TO TAKE OUR THOUGHTS CAPTIVE, quietness might be the hardest of all—sitting down, all alone, in the hush. At the same time, the one pattern that has been most useful for me is the practice of time alone with God, because the silence is where my thought life changed. And connection with God is the foundation for every other God-given tool we have in our arsenal. If supernatural change is what we want, we have to go to our supernatural God to find it.

And how exactly do we do that? The practice of stillness and solitude in the presence of God is the basis of our strategy for interrupting all kinds of problematic thought patterns. Consider how simply thinking about God can shift your spiraling thoughts. If, say, you're in a high-pressure situation at work, these thoughts might churn their way through your mind:

> *I'm upset because I was passed over for the promotion I deserved.*
>
> *I'm stressed because I'm working overtime yet not making ends meet.*

I'm anxious because I'm running behind on my project and letting people down.

I'm frustrated because my boss is a micromanager.

Notice the pattern in each of these thoughts: [Negative emotion] *because* [reason].

I'm stressed **because** *I'm working overtime.*

I'm angry **because** *she was rude.*

I'm frustrated **because** *I didn't keep my commitment to myself.*

I'm overwhelmed **because** *I have too much to do.*

With each tool God has given us to fight effectively in this battle for our minds, we get to rewrite that negative pattern while taking back the power He has given us. We can reframe our situations with a new pattern: [Negative emotion], *and* [reason], *so I will* [choice].[1]

I'm upset, **and** *I was passed over,* **so I will choose** *to remember that God has not forgotten me.*

I'm angry, **and** *she was rude,* **so I will choose** *to meditate on God's kindness toward me.*

---

1   For more on cognitive reframing, see Elizabeth Scott, "4 Steps to Shift Perspective and Change Everything," Verywell Mind, June 16, 2019, www.verywellmind.com/cognitive-reframing-for-stress-management-3144872.

I'm frustrated, **and** *I didn't keep my commitment to myself,* **so I will choose** *to look up verses on God's mercy toward me and how it's new every single day.*

I'm overwhelmed, **and** *I have too much to do,* **so I will choose** *to pause and thank God for existing outside the boundaries of time and for empowering me to accomplish only that which I* **need** *to do.*

When you're stuck in a downward spiral of distraction, to what truth will you shift your thoughts? How will you combat the lie that anything other than quieting yourself before God will truly satisfy you?

MEDITATE:
For God alone my soul waits in silence; from him comes my salvation. (Psalm 62:1)

REWIRE THE SPIRAL:
My heart was made to be still before God.

God, thank You for making it possible to rewrite the patterns in my brain. Ignite in me a craving for Your presence and teach me to choose You over and over again. Amen.

THE PATTERN

THERE'S A PATTERN AT WORK IN MANY OF US. OUR THOUGHTS ARE LEAD-ing us to emotions, and those emotions are dictating our decisions, and our decisions are determining our behaviors, and then our behaviors are shaping our relationships—all of which take us back either to healthy or unhealthy thoughts. Round and round and round we go, spinning down, seemingly out of control, all of it equaling the sum of our lives.

So many of us spend all our energy in conversations and counsel-ing and prayer, trying to shift the most visceral thing about us—our emotions—yet having no success. After all, if you're feeling sad and I tell you to quit feeling sad, has any progress been made? Not really. So it's time to try something different.

Instead of spending our energy trying to fix our symptoms, we should go straight to the root of the problem, deeper even than our emotions. The reality is that our emotions are a by-product of something else. Our emotions are a by-product of the way we think.

What's good about this news is that we can change our thinking. The Bible tells us so. In the book of Romans, the apostle Paul tells us we can be "transformed by the renewal of [our] mind" (12:2). And a deep dive into the inner workings of the brain confirms what the Bible says: Not only can our thoughts be changed, but we can be the ones to change them.

The enemy of our souls would have us think we are stuck the way we are. That the way we think is just "us," even if we don't like where it takes us. But God's truth tells us something different: We can, in fact, change. Science and the Bible confirm that we can interrupt our thoughts. Our brains are full of neuropathways, some shallow and some dug deep from a lifetime of thoughts, but all are moldable. In both cases, God is mighty to save. In both cases, He's mighty to heal.

You don't have to spin out in your thoughts. As you learn to interrupt your thoughts with God's truth, you will discover that He is after your freedom.

MEDITATE:
Do not be conformed to this world, but be transformed by the renewal of your mind, that by testing you may discern what is the will of God, what is good and acceptable and perfect. (Romans 12:2)

REWIRE THE SPIRAL:
I'm not a victim to my thoughts. I can interrupt them.

God, thank You for making me with the ability to change, and for fashioning my brain with the ability to rewire. When I feel stuck in my thoughts, lead me again toward Your truth. Amen.

ONE THOUGHT

GOD BUILT A WAY FOR US TO ESCAPE THE DOWNWARD SPIRAL THAT OUR thoughts tend to go into. But we rarely take it. We have bought the lie that we are victims to our thoughts rather than warriors equipped to fight on the front lines of the greatest battle of our generation: the battle for our minds.

The apostle Paul understood the war that takes place in our thoughts, how our circumstances and imaginations can become weapons that undermine our faith and hope. That's why he instructs us to "take every thought captive to obey Christ" (2 Corinthians 10:5).

Take *every* thought captive? Every one of them? Is that possible? Have you ever tried?

Is God serious?

Our thoughts run wilder than a hyperactive sparrow. Did you know that people have twelve to sixty thousand thoughts per day? And of those, 80 percent are negative, and 95 percent are repetitive thoughts from the day before?[1] Clearly the spiral is real and stuffed with more thoughts than it seems we can manage.

But what if, instead of trying to take every thought captive, you took just one thought captive?

What if one beautiful, powerful thought could shift this chaotic spiral of your life for the better . . . every time you thought it? What if you could grab hold of one truth that would shift the tempest of untruths that has left you feeling powerless over your brain?

One thought to think. Could you do that?

While we may not be able to take every thought captive in every situation we face every day, we can learn to take *one* thought captive and, in doing so, affect every other thought to come.

What's that thought?

I have a choice.

That's it.

I have a choice.

If you have trusted in Jesus as your Savior, you have the power of God in you to choose! You have a God-given, God-empowered, and God-redeemed choice regarding what you think about. You have a choice regarding where you focus your energy and what you live for.

I have a choice.

You are not subject to your behaviors, genes, or circumstances.

You are not subject to your passions, lusts, or emotions.

You are not subject to your thoughts.

---

1 Benjamin Hardy, "To Have What You Want, You Must Give-Up What's Holding You Back," Mission.org, June 9, 2018, https://medium.com/the-mission/to-have-what-you-want-you-must-give-up-whats-holding-you-back-65275f844a5a.

You have a choice because you are a conqueror who possesses weapons to destroy strongholds of the enemy in your life.

MEDITATE:
The weapons of our warfare are not of the flesh but have divine power to destroy strongholds. We destroy arguments and every lofty opinion raised against the knowledge of God, and take every thought captive to obey Christ. (2 Corinthians 10:4–5)

REWIRE THE SPIRAL:
I can grab one thought—I have a choice.

God, thank You for giving me a choice in what happens inside my head. Please remind me today to grab this one thought every time I feel my mind slipping into a spiral. I rely on Your divine power. Amen.

NOTICE YOUR THOUGHTS

A PSYCHIATRIST FRIEND OF MINE TOLD ME THAT MOST HUMANS BELIEVE
one of three basic lies that supply us with toxic thoughts. I couldn't believe it, because I felt like I was believing a million lies on any given day.
But she said, "Nope, just three." After I tested it out, it seemed pretty
feasible. Those lies are:

I am helpless.
I am unworthy.
I am unlovable.

These lies sit at the base of our spiraling fears.

Whatever your fear is, I'm not saying it's not real. There are so many
real problems right now—sickness, financial trouble, disastrous circumstances of all kinds. But until you get to the root of your fear, it will
continue to have a hold over you.

Let's try this. Take whatever problem triggers anxious feelings for
you, get a journal, and write down your thoughts daily. Start to notice

what it is you're worried about. Notice everything. Not just big, bad thoughts about things like losing your job, but every little thought about mundane worries. Some anxious thoughts you might not even notice until you write them down.

Once you get into a rhythm of recognizing your thoughts, you'll start to see a theme. That theme usually reveals something like, *What I'm really worried about is that I'm losing all my security.* The lie is, *I am helpless.* Whatever the "root" lie is, ask yourself where and when you started believing it. Then consider how you might be contributing to or perpetuating the lie. Hard stuff? Let's move on to the good part.

After you start to notice which lies you're believing, the next step is to put truth on it. If you're spiraling into an *I am unlovable* lie, you can't just say, "Untrue!" and will yourself into believing you're lovable. A lot of self-help approaches stop there, but this doesn't stick. God has more for us, and there is great hope in His plan and in His way of renewing our minds. While I might feel helpless, He is not. While I might feel unworthy, He has said I am worthy. While I might feel unlovable, He has said, "You're worth dying for."

What you dwell on in your mind will grow. So dig deep to discover the root of your anxious thoughts, and then replace it with truth. Believe truth, from the One who created you, who loves you, and who gives you help and hope. In this truth, you will be made free.

If you continue in My word,
then you are truly My disciples;
and you will know the truth,
and the truth will set you free.
(John 8:31–32, NASB)

I am strong, worthy, and loved
by the One who created me.

*Lord, reveal to me what lies I
might be believing, and teach
me to seek the truth that sets
me free. Amen.*

OUR ENEMY

IF WE BELIEVE THE BIBLE, WE MUST ACKNOWLEDGE THAT IT IS CLEAR ON one thing: There is an enemy to God and an enemy to us. We are at war—I don't know how else to say it. That enemy's desire is to kill, steal, and destroy. And one of the main ways I'm watching him do that in our generation is through our minds.

Jesus says that the enemy is the father of lies and that when he speaks, he lies—that is who he is. I have watched as person after person has believed these lies. I've believed them too. And here's the thing: We don't even realize we're believing lies. Eventually we start to believe they're true, and we consider them as accepted reality. Soon our minds become a mess, marked by discouragement, distraction, and exhaustion. But there's a way out.

The Bible says, "Though we walk in the flesh, we are not waging war according to the flesh" (2 Corinthians 10:3). We so often stop at the obvious things. We stop at the physical response and the emotional response rather than realizing there is another battle happening. And it is a spiritual war that is raging against us, in addition to the physical.

We all battle our own lies. And those lies are real to us. I've fallen under attacks so quiet and subtle that I totally forgot the enemy could be whispering a lie to me. I could believe a lie was true, walk in it, live with it, and build thought patterns and toxic spirals around it without ever recognizing the lie for what it was.

The enemy is cunning in how he uses certain lies to attack the minds of our generation. From cynicism to noise to victimhood, he's firing a volley of unique lies at us. Yet the weapons of warfare are not of the flesh but have divine power to destroy strongholds. By disciplining and training our thoughts, we can eventually, over time, change our minds.

You can recognize the enemy you're up against. You can speak with authority over the enemy's lies because of the power of God who is real and strong enough to destroy them. You can be free. Yes, there's an enemy. But our God is bigger.

MEDITATE:
Put on the whole armor of God, that you may be able to stand against the schemes of the devil. (Ephesians 6:11)

REWIRE THE SPIRAL:
The enemy is real, but my God is stronger.

God, thank You for Your power and Your protection. By Your Spirit, I pray that You would expose the lies of the enemy so I can live free. Amen.

LET'S FIGHT

THE GREATEST SPIRITUAL BATTLE OF OUR GENERATION IS BEING FOUGHT between our ears. This is the epicenter of the battle.

Every great or horrible act we see in history, in our children's lives, in our lives, is preceded by a thought. And that one thought multiplies into many thoughts that develop into a mindset, often without our even realizing it. Our goal is to be aware of our thoughts and to deliberately build them into mindsets that lead to the outcomes we want.

Just as one uninterrupted lie in my head has the potential to bring about unimaginable destruction in the world around me, **one God-honoring thought has the potential to change the trajectory of both history and eternity.**

In other words, you aren't what you eat. You aren't what you do. You are what you think.

You probably know what that one most recurring thought is for you, that one thought that more than any other informs your other thoughts and, yes, your actions. The enemy will tell you that change is hopeless, that you're a victim to your circumstances and your thought patterns.

The enemy wants you to settle, to find a way just to survive and be somewhat happy. The enemy will urge you to accept that "this is just who you are," that your thinking is rooted too deeply in your personality or your upbringing to ever shift.

Against such lies, your objective is to capture the toxic thought—to have the courage to face that defining, destructive thought—and interrupt it with this one: *I have a choice.* The point of taking every thought captive is not to take control ourselves of what happens to us but instead to rest in the truth that God is with us, is for us, and loves us even when all hell comes against us. Jesus defeated sin, Satan, and death and rose from the grave, and because of His victory, the same resurrection power indwells us who have been redeemed by the gospel.

This is a journey into joy that makes zero sense based on our circumstances.

This is a fight for clear, focused purpose amid rampant consumerism.

This is a God-given peace that surpasses understanding for our seasons of suffering.

This is redeeming the time amid unprecedented distraction and noise.

This is the beauty of esteeming others amid a narcissistic culture.

This is learning to speak the truth in love in a world that says we should never offend.

This is how you can breathe deeply and sleep peacefully in an anxiety-ridden society.

This is an otherworldly way to live.

You are a citizen of another reality. Let's learn to think like it.

As he thinks in his heart, so is he.
(Proverbs 23:7, NKJV)

REWIRE THE SPIRAL:
I choose to believe that God is
with me, is for me, and loves me.

*Jesus, You make the impossible
possible. You bring the power of
heaven to the darkness in this
world. Please redeem my mind;
I want to honor You with my
thoughts. Amen.*

THE MIND OF CHRIST

EVERY DAY WE'RE BOMBARDED WITH MESSAGES ABOUT HOW WE CAN do better and be better. We feel hope whenever we hear how the right mantra, workout, financial plan, or determination will lead us to a better, more fulfilling life. After all, who doesn't like that idea? None of us want to stay stuck where we are. We all want to flourish and thrive. Yet even with countless techniques to find happiness, we struggle to find one that will stick. Why? Because **for all the good that self-help does, that help always comes up short in the end. We need God-help.**

The best that self-help can do with our suffering, with our shortcomings, and with our spiraling is to declare, "Today this awfulness stops!" And great! So it should. But we don't simply need our spiraling thoughts to stop; we need our minds to be *redeemed*. Bondage necessitates rescue. Oppression needs to be lifted. Blindness waits for sight. Waywardness must be transformed. No self-generated declaration—loud and passionate though it may be—can do this. Instead, we need a complete transformation: our minds exchanged for the mind of Christ.

We were not made to think more good thoughts of ourselves. We were made to experience life and peace when we think less about ourselves and more about our Creator and about others. The only true self-help is for us as followers of Jesus to believe who we are as daughters and sons of the King of the universe and to know that our identity has been secured by the shed blood of God's own Son. When we believe that about ourselves, we think less about ourselves and more about loving God and the people God puts in front of us.

Sure, you can make progress on your own in getting out of your head. We can do a lot by ourselves to take control of our lives. We do have a part to play. But our effort won't take us across the finish line if there is no outside force shifting the inside of us.

Once you take a thought captive, you submit that thought to Christ. That's the only way you can experience a new mind, a new identity, and a new way to live—one that's Spirit indwelled and empowered. The world knows that no progress can be made without doing the work. But **self-help can offer only a better version of yourself; Christ is after *a whole new you*.** God in you. The mind of Christ.

MEDITATE:
"For who has understood the mind of the Lord so as to instruct him?" But we have the mind of Christ. (1 Corinthians 2:16)

REWIRE THE SPIRAL:
In Christ, my thoughts can be redeemed.

Jesus, I choose to believe Your powerful truths and to act on them today. Please transform and redeem my mind in the way only You can as I take my thoughts captive and bring them to You. Amen.

POWER AND AUTHORITY

CAPTURING ALL OUR THOUGHTS MIGHT SEEM AN IMPOSSIBLE TASK— especially when you consider we average more than forty thoughts per minute.[1] It all seems so out of control. But what if I told you that Christ has given us authority to interrupt our thoughts and send them where we want them to go?

Paul's own life was a picture of interruption. After the scales fell from his eyes, Paul's life and mind centered on an entirely new reality—one focused on God. There was no other hope, no other narrative, and no other track playing in the background. He stopped the things that had distracted him and let himself focus on one simple thing: "To me to live is Christ, and to die is gain" (Philippians 1:21). It's all—always—about Christ.

Paul experienced a massive shift and became a totally different man. No longer was he a slave to his circumstances or his emotions. Instead he chose to live aware of the power of Christ in him, through him, and for

---

1   "How Many Thoughts Do We Have per Minute?," Reference, www.reference.com/world-view/many-thoughts-per-minute-cb7fcf22ebbf8466.

him. Paul had the power of the Spirit, and he chose to live aware of and under that power.

In the late Eugene Peterson's paraphrase of Paul's words in The Message Bible, we read that we have that authority too:

> We use our powerful God-tools for smashing warped philosophies, tearing down barriers erected against the truth of God, fitting every loose thought and emotion and impulse into the structure of life shaped by Christ. Our tools are ready at hand for clearing the ground of every obstruction and building lives of obedience into maturity. (2 Corinthians 10:5–6, MSG)

Here's what I take from these words: You and I have been equipped with power from God to tear down the strongholds in our minds and to destroy the lies that dominate our thought patterns. We have the power and authority to do this! Yet we walk around acting as though we have no power over what we allow into our minds.

For too many years of my life, I was a victim to the negativity rising against me. Do you relate? Have you also spent way too much of your life handing over the power inside you to the arguments and lies in your head?

Paul tells us that we don't have to live this way, that we can take captive our thoughts. And in so doing, we can wield our power for good and for God, slaying strongholds left and right. We have the power and authority over our minds, not the other way around. How exciting is that!

MEDITATE:
For freedom Christ has set us free; stand firm therefore, and do not submit again to a yoke of slavery. (Galatians 5:1)

REWIRE THE SPIRAL:
In Christ's power, I have authority over my mind.

Jesus, please help me exercise the authority You've given me to interrupt my thoughts and center them on You. Amen.

SET YOUR MIND

WITH ALL WE KNOW ABOUT THE BRAIN TODAY, WE CAN SEE THAT EVERY reference in Scripture to the heart really is about the mind and the emotions we experience in our brains. So many of the truths in the Bible concerning our thought lives have been backed up by science. This all becomes increasingly important as we explore how taking control of our minds could be the key to finding peace in every other area of our lives.

We once thought of the mind as an immutable, given thing. The brain you were born with and the way it worked—or didn't—was just "how it was"; no sense fretting over what can't be changed. We now know that the brain is constantly changing, whether or not we intend for it to.

How does it change? Dr. Daniel Siegel writes, "Where attention goes, neural firing flows and neural connection grows. . . . Patterns you thought were fixed are actually things that with mental effort can indeed be changed."[1] In other words, we can choose where we deliberately place our attention and where we shouldn't place it.

---

1 Daniel J. Siegel, *Mind: A Journey to the Heart of Being Human* (New York: Norton, 2017), 179, 185.

Thankfully, what starts as effort becomes instinctual. What was only possible for me twelve months ago became probable a few months after that. And what was probable back in the springtime became predictable by summer's end. And based on Paul's insight in today's verse, you and I can learn to mind our minds to the point that controlling our thoughts becomes reflexive—an automatic, intuitive response.

How would your life change if you could truly adopt a mindset that dwells on the Spirit? A mindset that centers on life and peace? A mindset that consistently thinks about God—who He is and what He wants for you? This is the goal of deliberate interruptions: You can abruptly stop the crazy spirals of your mind. As you practice the art of interruption, you can shift to a whole new mindset, and with each shift find yourself growing more and more into the mind of Christ.

MEDITATE:
Those who live according to the flesh set their minds on the things of the flesh, but those who live according to the Spirit set their minds on the things of the Spirit. For to set the mind on the flesh is death, but to set the mind on the Spirit is life and peace.
(Romans 8:5–6)

REWIRE THE SPIRAL:
I will choose today to dwell on God's truth.

God, help me today to set my mind on the things of the Spirit—on life and peace. Thank You for giving me the ability to change and to set the direction of my thoughts on You. Amen.

IMAGINE JOY

BEFORE ANOTHER DAY PASSES IN THIS BATTLE FOR YOUR MIND, I WANT you to know that there is so much grace for this process. It is a day-by-day, minute-by-minute journey, with a lot of ups and downs. It might not feel worth it sometimes. It might feel like a bunch of mumbo jumbo. But I promise, it is worth it. Freedom is on the other side.

So I ask you, What does freedom look and feel like for you? What would a healthy, resilient, flourishing mind look like? What would you leave behind? What would you take up? When things get tough, I want you to imagine joy. Imagine a healthy day in which you get through the day and smile at the end of it, recognizing the peace you feel. When you have margin and space or connection with people you love. Imagine being advanced in years, being with your grandkids or other young ones, and being delightful, not bitter. Such is the fruit of a cultivated mind.

The thing with spirals is that they grow. Bitterness grows—but so does joy and peace and patience and kindness. So let's keep the long view in mind. That we want to get healthy for our families and grandkids and future generations. We want to get healthy for ourselves. We want to get healthy for our day-to-day life. If we have that in mind, then we won't give up so easily.

You know how not long after New Year's, all of us tend to fall off the wagon of our disciplines or resolutions? I fall off every single time. But I want to take the shame away from that. It's human. That's what we do. We fall off, and we get back up. We spiral, we fail, and then we get back up and choose to put some healthy rhythms back into our lives. We forget we have a choice, and then we remember. You just get up and do it again. And you know what? Over time, you will be a different person. You may not be different today, and you may not be different tomorrow, but one hundred days from now, or even years from now, as you put these patterns into practice and see the power that God has given you, you will be different. And life will become so much more delightful. So much more enjoyable. This is possible. God made it so.

MEDITATE:
Let us not grow weary of doing good, for in due season we will reap, if we do not give up. (Galatians 6:9)

REWIRE THE SPIRAL:
What I choose today is for the good of my future.

God, thank You for making me to change, remold, and rewire over time. When I fall, help me imagine and inhabit Your vision for my life—a vision of freedom and delight. Amen.

REDIRECT

WHAT DO YOU FIXATE ON?

You know your fixation. It is the thing you constantly think about. Our fixations come out in our words, in our feelings, and in our decisions. They are the focus of the books we read, the podcasts, websites, and groups we search out, and the obsessions we pursue. It might be your weight, or worries over your kids, or fear for your health. *Something* is absorbing your thoughts.

Here's the thing: *God has given you the power to interrupt this fixation!* That's what the Bible says to us, and it is news we desperately need to hear.

The question remaining is, How? How could I interrupt my downward spin?

For you, the answer, at least in part, might lie in counseling. Or in community. Or in fasting. Certainly, in prayer. For you and me both, the answer will center on God—on His presence, on His power, and on His grace.

Every spiral can be interrupted. No fixation exists outside God's long-armed reach.

He has given us the power and the tools and His Spirit to shift the spiral. When we're willing to take the initiative in choosing different thoughts and choosing His truth, some pretty cool stuff starts to unfold.

For one thing, when we think new thoughts, we physically alter our brains. We grow new neurons. We blaze new trails. When we think new thoughts, everything changes for us. What we think about, our brains become. What we fixate on is neurologically who we will be.

So who will you be? It all comes down to a thought. And then another thought. And then another thought after that. Tell me what you're thinking about, in other words, and I'll tell you who you are.

If we don't like where that's going, we have the power to redirect those thoughts. Like we do with kids when they start losing it. "Kiddo, time out," we tell them. "I love you. You're okay. You don't have to panic. You can choose another way. You don't have to be steamrolled by this."

We tell them what is real. What is true. And what's true for them is also true for us. We redirect children all the time. Why shouldn't we redirect ourselves?

First we have to remind ourselves that change is possible. We have a choice! And the more often we grab hold of that truth, the easier it will be to interrupt our fixations and the downward spiral of our thoughts— and lead them somewhere new.

You may find that some thoughts, once interrupted, will simply lose their power. God can do this. Other thoughts, however, may require daily capturing and redirecting. Or hourly. Or more often than that. But those thoughts can be captured. They can be contained.

You can be set free. You can learn to mind your mind. The battle for your mind is won as you redirect and refocus on Jesus—every moment, every hour, every day.

WASHED CLEAN

IN THE PROCESS OF THINKING ABOUT OUR THOUGHTS, WE WILL PROB-ably hit highs and lows. We might feel awesome and free one day and filled with shame the next. The thing to remember, though, is this: We are not defined by our worst or best; we are defined by our God.

All our inclinations to strive and prove ourselves point to our need to be rescued. Our greatest need begins to be filled when we admit we have great needs, and we turn to the only One able to meet them. Scripture tells us we have a God who is faithful to forgive our sins and cleanse us. He's a cleansing God. A healing God. It's terrifying to put it out there and admit our need. But you want to be on the other side of it, I promise. You want to be clean and free.

The Christian life can be summed up in three words: repent and believe. You confess all your sin, the worst of it, and you believe the truth of God. We agree with God about our sin, and we don't just confess it, but we also let the cleansing stream of Jesus's grace pull us away from our sin. This will take humility.

In my experience, humility usually involves a bit of humiliation. Every time I am honest about my struggles, my sin, my pride, the mistakes I've made, and the sin in my soul, I find it humiliating. And do you know what happens right after I confess it? I immediately feel all the things I don't want to feel—the shame, the fear, the isolation, the embarrassment. I do feel them for a minute. I feel caught.

I let that feeling wash over me because the next wave coming is relief. I actually get to be cleansed now, and the shame that inevitably had affected me and everyone around me starts falling off and recedes with the waves of grace. In the same way, when we confess our sins, we expose our dirt because Jesus has the power to wash it and free us from bondage to it. God's grace is exquisite and enough for the dirt that seems impossible to clean. Repent and believe.

This is what it looks like to fill your soul with what Jesus promises: streams of living water, bread that does not ever leave you hungry again, and light that takes over the darkness. So put out your dirt and let Jesus wash it, and then go tell everybody about what He has done.

MEDITATE:
If we say we have no sin, we deceive ourselves, and the truth is not in us. If we confess our sins, he is faithful and just to forgive us our sins and to cleanse us from all unrighteousness. (1 John 1:8–9)

REWIRE THE SPIRAL:
I am not defined by my worst or best. I am defined by God.

God, I'm so thankful that it's not all up to me to free myself. I want to be washed clean in the way only You can do. Please show me what it means to repent and believe. Amen.

EMOTION
Fear of a real or perceived threat

CONSEQUENCE
Unafraid

THOUGHT
I cannot trust God to take
care of my tomorrows

RELATIONSHIPS
Present and open

BEHAVIOR
Resistant to God's authority

BEHAVIOR
Submitted to God's authority

RELATIONSHIPS
Controlling and manipulative

THOUGHT
God is in control of every day
of my life

I choose to surrender ⟶

CONSEQUENCE
Constant anxiety

EMOTION
Fear of a real or perceived threat

FROM
ANXIETY
TO
SURRENDER

WHAT IF?

DO YOU EVER FIND YOURSELF DRAGGING THROUGH THE DAY, WEIGHED down by anxious thought patterns? Do you ever notice your thoughts circling around problematic circumstances or people? Has anxiety ever become your daily soundtrack, so familiar you hardly notice it playing in the background of every scene?[1]

No matter how anxiety plays out, the enemy tends to get the ball rolling by ensnaring us with two little words: What if? With them, he sets our imaginations whirling, spinning tales of the doom that lurks ahead: *What if I get too close to this person and she manipulates me like the last friend I trusted? What if my spouse cheats on me? What if my children die tragically? What if my boss decides I'm expendable? What if?*

As a culture, we are "what-if-ing" ourselves to death. Thankfully, our tool for defeating "what if" is, not surprisingly, also found in two words: Because God.

---

1   Please know that I'm talking here about thought patterns, not about anxiety that is rooted in your body's chemistry and for which I urge you to seek professional help, if this is your situation.

Because God clothes the lilies of the field and feeds the birds of the air, we don't need to be anxious about tomorrow.

Because God has poured His love into our hearts, our hope will not be put to shame.

Because God chose us to be saved by His strength, we can stand firm in our faith no matter what the day holds.

Freedom begins when we notice what is binding us. Then we can interrupt it with the truth.

Certainly there are healthy levels of what-if anxiety that signal our brains to be afraid of things that are truly worth being afraid of—such as a bear in the woods or oncoming traffic when we are crossing a street. But when our brains get stuck in the anxiety—a flight reaction when there's no bear in sight—that's a spiral waiting to happen. In those moments, our emotional reaction to scary things goes beyond rational to illogical, because our brains' fear networks are in overdrive.

Since constant stewing is no way to prepare yourself for the future, try to notice the moments when you tend to create new concerns to worry about. When you experience physical responses to situations or people who are not real threats, and your chest becomes tight, preventing you from being relaxed or fully present. In those moments, when your very worst nightmares come true—whether real or imagined—remind yourself that there is a God who will give you all you need.

The lie says, *I cannot trust God to take care of my tomorrows.* The truth is, *God is in control of every day of my life.*

Today you can choose to surrender your fears to God.

The very hairs on your head are all numbered. So don't be afraid; you are more valuable to God than a whole flock of sparrows. (Luke 12:7, NLT)

When the fear sets in, I can feel peace, "because God."

God, I want to notice what's going on in my heart and mind. Please help me remember the truth that You are in control when my mind starts spinning. Amen.

WHAT IS REAL

PAUL KNEW OUR THOUGHTS WOULD SPIRAL. THAT'S CLEAR FROM THE way he wrote his letter to the Philippians. Yet he says to them, "Do not be anxious about anything."

Anything?

Anything.

How could Paul say that? Does God really command this of us?

Well, Paul certainly had plenty to be anxious about. When he wrote those words, he was locked in prison with a death sentence on his head. Nonetheless, he meant what he wrote. He meant it for one simple reason: This earth is not our home, and our home in heaven is secure. So if death is not to be feared, what exactly do we have to be scared of?

God's promises give us ultimate hope in absolutely every circumstance. He meets every need. He will resolve (in the end) every problem we may face here on earth. Paul wrote in confidence of this truth, and then he gave us clear guidance for ridding ourselves of anxious thoughts. He wrote, "Finally, brothers and sisters, whatever is true, whatever is noble, whatever is right, whatever is pure, whatever is lovely, whatever is admirable—if anything is excellent or praiseworthy—think about such things" (Philippians 4:8, NIV).

Let's zero in on one of these replacement thoughts: "Whatever is true . . . think about such things."

What gets most of us in trouble aren't even real fears. We worry about things that may never happen. In fact, "Ninety-seven percent of what you worry over is not much more than a fearful mind punishing you with exaggerations and misperceptions."[1] Puts everything you worry about into perspective, doesn't it?

In the gospel of John, we find an incredible description of the enemy:

He was a murderer from the beginning, and does not stand in the truth, because there is no truth in him. When he lies, he speaks out of his own character, for he is a liar and the father of lies. (John 8:44)

In this passage, we see that truth is the most powerful weapon we have against the enemy, who is "a liar and the father of lies." So we fight the enemy with whatever is true—meaning, whatever is real!

You may be a natural worrier or someone who is more optimistic. But regardless of personality, God has called you to hope, to joy, to perseverance—to think on what is true!

---

1   Don Joseph Goewey, "85% of What We Worry About Never Happens," December 7, 2015, https://donjoseph goewey.com/eighty-five-percent-of-worries-never-happen-2, citing data summarized in Robert L. Leahy, *The Worry Cure: Seven Steps to Stop Worry from Stopping You* (New York: Three Rivers Press, 2005), 18–19.

MEDITATE:
Do not be anxious about
anything, but in every
situation, by prayer and
petition, with thanksgiving,
present your requests to
God. (Philippians 4:6, NIV)

REWIRE THE SPIRAL:
I can choose what is true over
what "might" happen.

*God, I trust You to reveal to me
what is real and what is true.
Please help me choose to weigh
my anxious thoughts against Your
truth, grabbing each one and
bringing it to You. Amen.*

WHAT DO I DO?

WHAT DO I DO?

I've heard countless people ask this question, people facing all sorts of challenges—cheating spouses and debilitating addictions and failed financial ventures and wayward kids and devastating diagnoses. Each time, after they explain what is sending them spinning, they ask that same question: "What do I do?"

What they're wondering is what they should do to fix the situation. Or to fix their perspective. Or to keep pain and suffering at bay. Or if none of those things are a possibility, they want me to tell them how in the world they keep moving forward without giving in to desperation and despair.

What do I do?

Psst. Let me tell you the greatest news: You are not God. You are not omniscient.

When we allow our thoughts to spin out of control with worry and fear, either consciously or unconsciously we try to elbow our way into the all-knowing role that only God can play. We forget that it's actually good news that He is in control and we are not. You and I may have many gifts and talents, but being God is not one of them.

Our job is to rely on God and embrace His control. Even in the face of our fears.

When you recognize the lie that the whole world is resting heavy on your shoulders, you can take off that suffocating coat and set it aside.

So what do you do when you start to spin? You remind yourself who God is and cast your anxieties on Him. You may have to do this a hundred times a day. And you claim the peace of God as your promise.

What fear-filled thought is Satan using to suffocate your faith? Say its name. And search for the truth.

○ *I'm afraid that I won't be able to withstand whatever the future might hold.* **Rely on God, who will not allow you to be tempted beyond what you can bear and will always give you the strength to bear temptation (1 Corinthians 10:13).**

○ *I'm afraid that everyone will abandon me.* **Rely on God, who promises not to leave you and always keeps His promises (Deuteronomy 31:8).**

○ *I'm afraid of failing miserably for everyone to see.* **Rely on God, who specializes in taking weakness and using it for His glory (2 Corinthians 12:9–10).**

This is how we fight the spiral. We pull the thoughts out of our heads, we steal all their power, and then we replace them with what is true!

MEDITATE:

The LORD is my light and my salvation; whom shall I fear? The LORD is the stronghold of my life; of whom shall I be afraid? (Psalm 27:1)

REWIRE THE SPIRAL:

I can trust God and His truth when I don't know what to do.

God, when I don't know what to do, help me remember that You are in control and able to catch me in all my fears. Amen.

ANXIOUS FOR NOTHING

IT TAKES FAITH TO BELIEVE GOD IS GOOD AND PERFECT, EVEN WHEN life is not. And it takes an active choice to believe He is in control.

I want to tell you a hard truth: There are no promises that our worst fears won't come true. Sometimes they do, but even then, God remains our unfailing hope. Cancer may afflict us or those we love, yet by God's power, it will not win, at least not in the end. A spouse may be unfaithful, yet by God's power, infidelity won't define our lives. Financial crisis may come against us, yet by God's power, we can move forward. Disillusionment and doubt may overwhelm us, yet by God's power, they won't have the last word.

Corrie ten Boom's book *The Hiding Place* tells the story of a Dutch family who hid Jewish families during the Holocaust. As I read it, I wrestled with the parts of her story that propose that no matter what the future holds for us, God is enough. Corrie related this moment in the book:

Father sat down on the edge of the narrow bed. "Corrie," he began gently, "when you and I go to Amsterdam—when do I give you your ticket?"

I sniffed a few times, considering this.

"Why, just before we get on the train."

"Exactly. And our wise Father in heaven knows when we're going to need things, too. Don't run out ahead of Him, Corrie. When the time comes that some of us will have to die, you will look into your heart and find the strength you need—just in time."[1]

With God, we always have exactly what we need, when we need it. Do you believe that?

This kind of faith is what helps us develop the mind of Christ: a mind that trusts the Father to give us exactly the strength we need, and doesn't get ahead of Him by focusing on how our worst fears might come true.

Please hear me: No matter how your life looks today, no matter what tomorrow holds, God does care for you. You are seen and cared for, and there is nothing to fear, because God has you. You don't have to run out ahead of Him with your anxieties. He will give you the strength you need, when you need it most.

1   Corrie ten Boom, *The Hiding Place* (New York: Bantam Books, 1974), 29.

God is my salvation; I will trust, and will not be afraid; for the LORD GOD is my strength and my song, and he has become my salvation. (Isaiah 12:2)

God will give me what I need when I need it.

God, when I fear for the future, show me again how firmly You have me. Fill me with faith and trust in Your power, and remind me that You can make all things right, no matter what comes. Amen.

FEARING GOD

WHEN GOD'S WORD TELLS US, *DO NOT FEAR ANYTHING IN THIS WORLD,* it is because God has us. It is because nothing is going to come against us, not even the enemy, without God's permission. God has in His hand every circumstance you face. God understands the spirals, the fears you're feeling, and the doubts you're experiencing. He understands and knows about all of it, and He's powerful over it.

We cannot completely guard our lives from the bad things happening. That's not possible. That's not the goal in this world. We will have trouble, God says. Bad things have happened to godly people and will continue to do so until Jesus comes back. But the reality of the wrong and terrible in the world doesn't mean we have to live in fear. A life of fear is not what Jesus died for. He gave up His own life so that we can live *free* from fear. Of course, because we live in a fallen world, we will wrestle with real fears. But in the face of those fears, we can remember that we have an eternal hope.

That's what Luke is talking about in today's verse. He doesn't diminish the enemy or his fear tactics, but he does say, *Don't be afraid of death.*

Don't be afraid of sickness. Don't be afraid of suffering here. If you're going to be afraid of something, be afraid of the One who can send you to hell. He's saying, *Make sure your eternity is secure. The only lasting thing that can be taken from you is eternity. Everything else can be redeemed. It can be used for good. It can be worked into this eternal story. But make sure God is in His right place.*

Fearing God is respecting His power. And as A. W. Tozer says, once we have God in His rightful place, a thousand problems are solved all at once.[1] When God is in His right place, our fear shifts from life-sucking fear of the world to life-giving fear of God. This is the fear that makes us free.

MEDITATE:
I tell you, my friends, do not fear those who kill the body, and after that have nothing more that they can do. But I will warn you whom to fear: fear him who, after he has killed, has authority to cast into hell. Yes, I tell you, fear him! (Luke 12:4–5)

REWIRE THE SPIRAL:
Because Jesus is my salvation, my eternity is secure, no matter what happens on earth.

God, even if my worst fears come true, I choose to surrender. You are the Almighty God. You have my life and my days in Your hands, and I will trust You. Amen.

---

1   A. W. Tozer, *The Pursuit of God* (1957; reprint: Camp Hill, PA: WingSpread, 2007), 97.

A SINGLE-MINDED HOPE

IN HIS LETTER TO THE CORINTHIANS, PAUL WRITES TO THE CHURCH about what he calls his "light and momentary" trials. But he's not talking about a traffic jam or a stubbed toe here. He's talking about being shipwrecked, nearly killed, imprisoned, and beaten—some of the worst stuff that can happen. Why is he speaking of these things as "light and momentary"? Because he has a view of eternity that is so real and palpable to him. He knows he's in the first opening scene of eternity, that "now" is just a short part of his life. And he's not going to be derailed by the only power the enemy has, which is of *right now.*

Currently in this world, the enemy still has some power. He doesn't have victorious power. He's not going to win in the end. But right now, God allows the enemy to bring attack against us for a season, knowing that this time will end.

The book of Revelation promises that there will be a time when the enemy is cast away and kept from the people of God, and that suffering and death and darkness will no longer be a part of our story and a part of our lives, because God will deal with it forever. And that time is coming.

But in this time, God in His mercy is holding back His hand, because at the time of justice, at the time of judgment, He doesn't want people to perish (2 Peter 3:9).

And so, yes, we are aching to be with God one day, but we have work to do in the meantime. As long as history is still turning and the earth is still spinning, we have work to do here. Paul's mentality was, *I'm not going to get distracted by the difficulty. I'm not going to live paralyzed by the fear that it will happen. It will happen. I won't be surprised by it, but I will live with hope in an eternity that will be greater than anything I deal with here.*

There was a hope in heaven and eternity that was far bigger for Paul than any other thing in his life. I don't know about you, but I want that. I want to emulate that. He even said, "follow my example, as I follow the example of Christ" (1 Corinthians 11:1, NIV). And as we follow him, what we find is a single-mindedness that provides an escape route from fear. It's a way out, because what grips those of us in fear is that we might lose something on earth. Yet Paul knew, *I'm going to lose things on earth. I'm going to live like Christ if I'm alive. And Christ lost His life, Christ lost friends, Christ was betrayed—Christ lost. So I'm going to lose on earth.*

That's what he meant when he said, "To me to live is Christ, and to die is gain" (Philippians 1:21). Death is a gain because that's where everything is reconciled. That's the kind of hope that turns fear on its head. So you don't have to be afraid of what you might lose on this earth, because you have the hope of heaven.

This light momentary affliction is preparing for us an eternal weight of glory beyond all comparison, as we look not to the things that are seen but to the things that are unseen. For the things that are seen are transient, but the things that are unseen are eternal. (2 Corinthians 4:17–18)

Hope in the eternal puts my fears in their place.

God, I want to keep sight of eternity and what awaits me there. Place on my heart the weight of Your glory and Your goodness that outweighs the light and momentary things of this earth. Amen.

FEED YOUR FAITH

OUR WEAPON AGAINST FEAR IS TRUST IN GOD. CLAIMING THAT TAKES effort. It takes fighting for belief. My hope is that we would fight for our faith, that we would prize it, and that we would realize that waiting on God and trusting in God contains great reward.

Over the years, I have watched Him come through again and again. My own trust has grown from the time I first knew God, and I no longer stand trembling about what might happen to my kids or my husband. But if I think about it too long, I will. So I don't feed that. I don't give energy to that. I interrupt it. I redirect it. I don't throw gas on the fire. Why? Because why give something that dark my energy? When God has not asked me to face that trial or that dreadful event today, why would I feed the fear that comes from it?

One day I might have to face my fears come true. Something could happen to somebody I love dearly, my husband, my kids. Something bad will happen to us one day, and I will have to face that. But I know on that day I will have what I need. So today I don't feed that fear.

Are you feeding fear? What fear are you feeding, and how can you interrupt it? How can you use the weapons in your arsenal? God has given you powerful weapons like His Word and the community around you. How can you embrace those things and let them help you build your trust, depend on Him more, and not let this fear take you out?

Because fear will try to take you out. It will try to distract and derail you. It will attempt to keep you from being bold, from experiencing joy, and from knowing peace.

But God has given you power over fear to say, "No more. Am I going to dwell on this? Am I going to feed it? Am I going to give energy to this? No." Interrupt the thoughts. Choose to believe God's truth on a daily basis. Stop the spiral—because you can.

At the point where that fear enters your mind, you can confess it. You can bring it to God. You can express it to your people, and you can interrupt it. Funnel your energy toward these things—because you have a choice. And faith is a choice that brings us so much freedom.

MEDITATE:
I have said these things to you, that in me you may have peace. In the world you will have tribulation. But take heart; I have overcome the world. (John 16:33)

REWIRE THE SPIRAL:
I can choose the thoughts I feed and where I direct my energy.

Jesus, today I choose faith in You. Help me direct my time and energy to things that bring life and cut them off from things that don't. Amen.

DAY
21

WORKING THROUGH WORRIES

LET'S GET PRACTICAL. WHAT IS WORRYING YOU THE MOST? WHAT IS giving you the most anxiety? Write down some of those thoughts, and then choose one. Let's work through it together step by step.

First ask, *Is it true?* Is the thing you're worried about even real?

I worked through this process myself, and the thing I was worried about most was my son having just left for college. I was fretting: Is he going to make good decisions? Is he going to date girls I like? Before I knew it, in my imagination, I was fearing that he somehow would end up in prison. Now this is pretty far-fetched. At the moment, my son loves God and is making good choices. And he's a great kid. Why was I so worried that he's going to derail his life? My fears were not based on reality.

But even if they were—and maybe for you, something like this actually is true—there is still hope. If your fear is true, what next?

The next question is, *What does God's Word say about it?* For one thing, the Bible says there is redemption in all things—because of hope and the power of God to take things that are broken and turn them into things that are beautiful. That is the continued story of redemption and how God works. We have hope in all things. There's no situation we don't have hope in, because He works all things together for good. That is what Scripture tells us. So even if something we're worrying about is real, we can ask, *What does God say about it?* And then we can begin to say things like, "You know what? He is working all things together for good. Heaven is coming. And I have a home with Him forever." We just start pinpointing what's true.

The last question we ask is, *Am I going to believe God?* That's the real question. If you're like me, you can work through the question of whether it's true or false without a problem. You can search out what God's Word says. But then *choosing* to believe that truth on a daily basis? That's where the enemy gets you. That's where you can choose better. So often we keep believing the lie, acting on it, and letting the what-ifs stir our thoughts into a frenzy. But you have the choice to believe God. And when you work through this process from beginning to end, again and again, you'll begin to see what freedom from fear looks like.

MEDITATE:

We know that for those who love God all things work together for good, for those who are called according to his purpose. (Romans 8:28)

REWIRE THE SPIRAL:

I can untangle the chaos of my mind and find peace in God's truth.

Father, when You tell me all things work together for good, let me not gloss over that truth. Let it soak deeply within my soul. As I work through my worries, help me choose to believe Your promises. Amen.

LOSS AND GAIN

I HAVE A FRIEND WHO, BECAUSE OF VARIOUS HEART CONDITIONS, HAS faced death many times, and whose broken heart could take her to heaven at any moment. If I were her, I'd be beset with anxiety and fear. But she amazes me with the peace she has in Jesus. At the core of my friend isn't a fear of death; it is an ache for heaven.

If we could actually believe that on the other side of this life are the best parts, then what would we have left to fear? If we could believe that we have nothing to fear even in death, I'm convinced we could get on with living. There would still be trials. There would still be suffering. However, if we could quit being so afraid of dying, we could start to live.

But as long as we grasp for our lives, trying to control them, we are losing them. We all have dreams for our lives, for our kids, for our careers, for our ministries, for our friendships. We have expectations of how our lives will turn out. Yet even if many of your dreams come true, they'll never fill your soul like you thought they would. This life is not enough to fill us, but Jesus is so completely sufficient that it doesn't matter.

Many people who have suffered the most also contain the most joy. Jesus calls us to this backward way of life. Dreams here can be shattered, or our best dreams can be realized, yet compared to the surpassing glory of knowing Christ, we can consider everything a loss. As the apostle Paul says, in essence, "I consider the dreams here, both those disappointed and those achieved, garbage, that I may gain Christ and be found in Him."[1]

Those of us who have Jesus can be free from worry about this life working out perfectly, because a perfect eternal life is coming. Who or what on this earth would we fear if God is with us? Death? Jesus defeated it. Pain? It comes to an end. So we can stop being so afraid. Because our eternity is safe if we have Jesus, fear has no power over us. And nothing else in this world does either.

MEDITATE:
I count everything as loss because of the surpassing worth of knowing Christ Jesus my Lord. For his sake I have suffered the loss of all things and count them as rubbish, in order that I may gain Christ and be found in him. (Philippians 3:8)

REWIRE THE SPIRAL:
In light of my eternal future with Christ, fear has no power over me.

Jesus, please shift my perspective. Let my hope in You be all-surpassing and help me choose to count all things as loss compared to You. Your love is infinitely sufficient. Amen.

---

1   See Philippians 3:8–9.

GRACE FOR THE UNTHINKABLE

WHEN FEAR OVERWHELMS US, WE NEED TO REMEMBER WHAT WE BE-lieve. Do you believe the Bible is true? That Jesus has gone before us and is building a home for us? Do you believe this is a story you're a part of? Do you believe God is more powerful than every single thing you fear? That's faith.

I can't tell you that your fears won't come true. I can't. But I can tell you I have lived long enough, been through enough, and seen people I love go through enough that I can promise you this: On the day when something unthinkable happens, you will have more grace from God to deal with it than you can possibly imagine.

Right now, you maybe don't have that grace, but I have seen it again and again and again: On that day He will give you everything you need to go through it. So don't fear. Not because it won't be hard. But it's pos-sible to walk through the darkest nights when we have a hope that lasts forever. We have a God who not only tells us, *Have hope,* but also adds, *I will walk through this with you, and I will be in it with you. I will provide things you can't even imagine on that day.*

I don't understand why bad things happen to good people. I don't have the answer for that. I can just tell you that I know there is a good God who's more powerful than all of it, and that one day we will all understand, even though we may not understand here.

So how do we not fear? How do we not have anxiety? Well, we start by making sure our view of God is right. And that happens by knowing Him intimately, walking with Him regularly, knowing His Word, and knowing who He is. And it starts also by feeding ourselves truths and reality instead of lies.

So many of my fears and feelings are based largely not on what is real but on made-up narratives in my head. So you and I have to remember, what *is* real?

God is real. He is not going anywhere, even if your mind jumps to all kinds of dark places. You can't rely on your thoughts or feelings to hold your faith in place. God holds your faith in place.

MEDITATE:
Even though I walk through the valley of the shadow of death, I will fear no evil, for you are with me; your rod and your staff, they comfort me. (Psalm 23:4)

REWIRE THE SPIRAL:
God is with me and beside me, and He will never abandon me.

God, thank You for being my provider, and for walking with me no matter what I face. I trust You to hold me, whatever comes my way. Amen.

AT WAR

FEELING CONFUSED OR OVERWHELMED LATELY? IT HELPS TO REMEMBER: We are at war—and one of the enemy's greatest tools is confusion. So let me remind you of the problem we face and the mission we embrace.

Every enemy of our minds traces back to a core problem, which is that a battle is being waged for our lives. Standing between us and victory is one of three barriers—or perhaps all three: the devil, our wounds, and our sin.

Sometimes attack comes directly from Satan, and his strategy is obvious. He tempts with evil and punishes with suffering. Usually, however, he is sneaky. He tempts with successes and hypnotizes with comforts until we are numb to and apathetic about all that matters.

Sometimes the battle happens because we live in a fallen world. Circumstances befall us constantly that scream, "Things are not as they should be!" Yet we tend to carry around deep hurt from our brokenness, rarely noticing it, and never dealing with it or healing from it.

But mostly the trouble we face in this life takes the form of sin. Specifically our sin—as in the stuff we do or don't do.

Most of the time, you and I won't be taken down by a massive demonic attack. Our own small choices are accomplishing everything the devil intends—our passivity and destruction—with zero effort on his part. Whichever thing comes against us, though, the bottom line is that we are at war!

To defend ourselves during this battle, we need to name the specific enemies we each are facing. When we employ the right weapons at the right time to overcome the enemy, we can enjoy renewed intimacy with Jesus and walk in greater freedom than we have before.

Whew. Big task. Thankfully for us: *big God.*

So name the lies that threaten you. Learn to spot the signs that you've been sucked into the enemy's trap. Learn to fight the war against your mind. See what happens when you choose to shift your thoughts to God, to the truth of who He is, and to the truth of who you are because of Him. Seize things like community, service, and gratitude as you live out the truth. And because of God, you will stand victorious in the end.

MEDITATE:
We do not wrestle against flesh and blood, but against the rulers, against the authorities, against the cosmic powers over this present darkness, against the spiritual forces of evil in the heavenly places. (Ephesians 6:12)

REWIRE THE SPIRAL:
I can use the weapons God gives to win this fight.

God, You are the only one big enough to win this battle. Teach me to fight with wisdom and not live afraid of the enemy's schemes. I trust You to defend me. Amen.

EMOTION

Discontent

THOUGHT

I'll feel better if I
stay distracted

BEHAVIOR

Constant inputs

RELATIONSHIPS

Needy and frantic

CONSEQUENCE

Insecure

CONSEQUENCE

Secure

RELATIONSHIPS

Calming and reassuring

BEHAVIOR

Prayer and meditation

THOUGHT

Only being with God will satisfy me

I choose to be still ⟶

EMOTION

Discontent

FROM
DISTRACTION
TO
STILLNESS

KNOW THE TRUTH

WE LIVE IN THE NOISIEST GENERATION THAT HAS EVER EXISTED. NO generation has had to deal with more inputs than ours, from the phones in our hands to the screens in front of us to the voices filtering through our headphones. Still, in the onslaught, all of us have a choice when we wake up in the morning. Do we let ourselves get swept away by the noise? Or do we reach for something better?

It's urgent that you spend time with Jesus in His Word. Because you are at war, and you need the truth in your mind.

First, you need to know who you are in Christ. You need to know who God is. You need to know the point of your life before you head into it every day. You need to have truth so clearly before you that when you see and hear other inputs coming your way, and when you're faced by all the noise, you can sort out the truth from the lies.

This noise flooding our lives isn't random. This noise is feeding us lies—ideas about our worth, what we need to be happy, and our relationships. It's not just subtle background noise or elevator music. It's delivering an intentional message, and most of it is plain untrue.

When the truth is set before our minds completely clearly, we can counter the noise. God wants time with us—and not just so we know more facts about Him, but so we can fight better. So we can actually live the things we know about God. But we have to know those things first. And as we seek that knowledge, we'll see that He is fighting for us through His Word.

The Bible says that His Word is a two-edged sword, that it cuts through bone and pierces our souls (Hebrews 4:12). There's nothing else that has the power to do that. The Word of God can change us. It will never return void but will instead enter us and accomplish His purposes for us (Isaiah 55:11).

Spending daily time in the Word is so important, because connection with God is the foundation for every other God-given tool. You cannot know God, give God, rest in God, or find hope in God without time with Him. Time in the Word is how you can know more of God. And in the face of all the noise, the choice to take that time has real power.

MEDITATE:
The word of God is living and active, sharper than any two-edged sword, piercing to the division of soul and of spirit, of joints and of marrow, and discerning the thoughts and intentions of the heart.
(Hebrews 4:12)

REWIRE THE SPIRAL:
I can choose to spend time in the truth of God's Word.

God, thank You for fighting for me through Your Word. Thank You for the truth and clarity it brings. Today help me notice the noise in my life and counter it with the truth of Your Word. Amen.

ESCAPE INTO BUSYNESS

THERE ARE SO MANY WAYS WE AVOID SILENCE, SO MANY TYPES OF noise we choose to fill the gaping voids in our souls. Social media is just the obvious one. We keep music playing in the car or streaming through our headphones. We pack our schedules with all the good things we think we should be doing. We juggle committees and demanding jobs and try to keep up with an unrealistic number of friends—yet we feel isolated. We often do so much for God that we barely meet with Him. As a result, we feel as though we are losing everywhere we look.

Amid all this busyness, we've made it impossible to hear His voice saying, "Be still, and know that I am God" (Psalm 46:10).

And why are we filling our schedules to the max and doing everything we can to stay busy? What is it we are running or hiding from? What keeps us from carving out space and time for the quiet we so desperately need?

Ready for it?

We are afraid of being found out.

Just like Adam and Eve in the Garden of Eden, we find ourselves naked and afraid in life, and so we choose to hide. We fear being put to work or asked to do something hard. We fear being asked to change or give something up. And most frightening, we fear being alone. Quiet time isn't so quiet, is it? Our heads actually get noisier when the noise all around us falls away.

But behind every one of these fears is a lie: *I cannot face God as I am.*

Here's the truth: We are messed up, every one of us. Which is exactly why we need time with God alone, in the quiet, where we can hear His healing voice. We have a choice between chaos and quiet, between noise and solitude with God, between denial and healing.

The antidote to running from ourselves is running to the only One who helps us get over ourselves. The lie is that we will be shamed. **The truth is that the God who is Creator and sovereign over the universe and the God who conquered sin and death is the same God who wants to be with you in your pain, shame, and other circumstances.**

We forget that God not only loves us but actually likes us too. Yep, He sees all; He knows every thought before we think it.[1] And somehow, unlike humans, He has grace for all.

It's a lie that you'll feel better if you stay distracted. The truth is, only being with God will satisfy you.

---

1   Psalm 139:2, NCV.

MEDITATE:
Be still, and know that I am God.
(Psalm 46:10)

REWIRE THE SPIRAL:
God likes me and wants a
relationship with me.

*God, I choose to be still with
You. Thank You for loving me as
I am, and for wanting to be with
me. Draw my heart to You in the
quiet today. Amen.*

ATTEND TO HIM

WE WERE PHYSICALLY BUILT FOR SILENCE. GOD DESIGNED US THIS WAY, and science confirms that design. Quiet meditation quite literally changes and physiologically alters our brains.[1] It rewires our imaginations.[2] It decreases anxiety and depression.[3] It makes our brains stay younger longer.[4] We have fewer wandering thoughts.[5] And silence eventually shifts our perspectives.[6]

When we turn our thoughts from our problems to the only One who holds the solution in His hands, we gain wisdom we'd not otherwise

---

1   Barbara Bradley Hagerty, "Prayer May Reshape Your Brain," NPR, May 20, 2009, www.npr.org/templates/story/story.php?storyId=104310443.

2   Sam Black, *The Porn Circuit: Understand Your Brain and Break Porn Habits in 90 Days* (Owosso, MI: Covenant Eyes, 2019), 38, www.covenanteyes.com/resources/heres-your-copy-of-the-porn-circuit.

3   Cary Barbor, "The Science of Meditation," *Psychology Today,* May 1, 2001, www.psychologytoday.com/us/articles/200105/the-science-meditation.

4   Alice G. Walton, "7 Ways Meditation Can Actually Change the Brain," *Forbes,* February 9, 2015, www.forbes.com/sites/alicegwalton/2015/02/09/7-ways-meditation-can-actually-change-the-brain/#98deead14658.

5   Walton, "7 Ways."

6   Charles F. Stanley, "How to Meditate on Scripture," In Touch Ministries, August 3, 2015, www.intouch.org/Read/Blog/how-to-meditate-on-scripture.

know. We gain insight we'd not otherwise sense. We find One who is *willing* and *able* to help us and thus uniquely poised to intervene.

We come to see things not as they seem to us but as they truly are.

So what's the difference between how things seem and how they are? Ask this: How many times have you created entire storylines based on worst-case scenarios? Have you ever built an entire narrative that begins to take on a life of its own, based on assumptions and your overactive imagination—all because you attended to fears, distractions, and catastrophizing?

If the most valuable asset you possess is your attention, to what are you attending?

Are you attending to your fear? Or to the God who promises to be with you? Are you attending to your doubt? Or to the truth that never changes? Are you attending to your need for control? Or to God's plan for you even if chaos breaks into the present reality? Are you attending to how you compare with others? Or to the gratitude you have for all God has done for you? Are you attending to worries regarding your health, your bank account, your career, your spouse, your children, your regrets, your past? Or are you attending to the living God?

You can do one or the other, but you can't do both at the same time. Either you will attend to the things that are crushing you or you will take up the light burden that is Christ's. "Come to me," He says. "You don't have to do this alone."

Come to me, all who labor and are heavy laden, and I will give you rest. Take my yoke upon you, and learn from me, for I am gentle and lowly in heart, and you will find rest for your souls. For my yoke is easy, and my burden is light. (Matthew 11:28–30)

Stillness with God rewires my perspective.

Jesus, I want to attend to You. Help me return to You again and again and know the gentle rest You bring when I get quiet in Your presence. Amen.

GOD FIGHTS FOR US

DO YOU KNOW HOW GOOD IT FEELS TO HAVE SOMEONE FIGHT FOR you? To know someone has your back, is defending you, and will never give up on you?

God fights for us in a way we often overlook: in His Word. That's how He is fighting for you right now. Some of us look at that big Bible on the shelf and feel burdened by it. We might think, *Oh, reading the Bible is an obligation. I have to do it. But I've got so much else to do right now. . . .* The reality is, that Book is God fighting for you. He's fighting for you to be freer—fighting for you to know Him and His love for you more. He's fighting for you to understand how much He has done and wants to do for you. That's what that Book is, and that's what comes through in those words.

When we recognize the truth of what the Bible is, we can start to build a better relationship with God. Bible reading is not about us checking a task off a list or doing our Bible homework to get an A on some spiritual report card. It's looking at God's powerful Word in wonder and thinking, *Gosh, my God is there. I want to be with Him. I want to know Him.*

The Bible says, "A day in your courts is better than a thousand elsewhere" (Psalm 84:10). Do we believe that? Do we believe that time with God is better than any other place we could be? It's the only place I have ever felt true peace. In the quiet, with God—especially amid difficulty, and even amid mourning or anxiety or worry—the peace comes. And it stays as we continue steeping in His Word, letting it break old ways off us and replace lies with truth.

Will you allow God to fight for you? You can do that when you believe truth and realize the power of what you're allowing into your mind. Whether or not you're choosing them, inputs are coming at you all day, every day. You can decide how you respond to them.

So dig deep into Scripture today, choosing truth and reading it over yourself and your loved ones. Fight for yourself, fight for your people, and let God fight for you through His living, powerful Word.

MEDITATE:
The LORD will fight for you, and you have only to be silent.
(Exodus 14:14)

REWIRE THE SPIRAL:
God is fighting for me in His Word.

God, thank You for fighting for me—for giving me the power and peace that come in Your presence with Your Word. When I reach for it today, soak Your truth into my soul. Amen.

GOD LIKES YOU

SO MANY OF US WISH WE COULD JUST GET OUT OF OUR HEADS SOME-times. But we don't want to get out of our heads into nothingness—we can't. The reason to get out of our heads is so that we can get into a relationship with God.

When we fix God in the center of our minds, we experience a new kind of accountability. Because guess what? God knows every thought we think before we think it. We have a God who knows our thoughts already. He's in our thoughts *with* us. And while that brings some accountability, it also brings companionship. We are not alone, lost, or wandering in our own thoughts. God is with us in them, and He's not angry at us about them. He just desperately wants us to be free of the lies we are choosing to believe.

I get it if the thought of God being in your head with you is slightly unnerving. You might feel as though you're being watched by the thought police, or as though God is somehow disapproving of the things that run through your mind. Well, you might already know this, but just in case you forgot, God likes you. He *really* likes you. You're His kid. It's like my eleven-year-old son in the morning, when he has been a brat the day before or gotten in trouble. When he's coming down for breakfast and turns the corner into the kitchen, all I feel when I look at him is how much I like him. I *like* him. I don't just love him. I don't just need him to do something for me. In fact, I don't need that at all. I genuinely enjoy him just for who he is.

I think that's the thing we miss about God—how much He likes us. Yes, He's fighting for us. Yes, He loves us. Yes, He sent His Son to die for us, but He also delights over us. If you fixate on that, you'll desire more and more to be with that God. You'll want to enjoy Him. You'll want to spend time with Him in the quiet and let Him speak love to your heart. You'll want to experience His delight over you, and you'll want to be with Him.

So don't think of being known in your thoughts as a disciplinary action. It's actually the fullness of joy, being together with the One who made you for His own delight.

MEDITATE:
He brought me out into a broad place; he rescued me, because he delighted in me. **(Psalm 18:19)**

Thank You, God, for getting me. Teach me what it means to delight in You as You do in me. Amen.

REWIRE THE SPIRAL:
I am safe with God. He likes me and wants a relationship with me.

THE FULLNESS OF JOY

JOY IS DEFINED AS "THE EMOTION OF GREAT DELIGHT OR HAPPINESS caused by something exceptionally good or satisfying." By contrast, the definition of *entertainment* is "an agreeable occupation for the mind; diversion; amusement."[1] Seems pale in comparison, right?

We were made for wonder and joy, but too often we settle for mere entertainment. God created us to crave true, fulfilling joy. But for many of us, the longing to satisfy our hearts has driven us past God Himself—who was meant to be the fulfillment of those desires—and toward distraction and meager substitutes that dull the ache of dissatisfaction and disappointment but never truly fill us.

One of my favorite worship songs is called "Jesus Is Better." Think about that: *Jesus is better.* Better than every other pleasure on earth. Better than being in love. Better than the comfort of a beautiful home. Better than a month-long beach vacation. Better than an incredible meal. Better than shopping. Better than being liked. Better than a dream job. Better than sex.

I think I want to believe that. I know I'm supposed to. But on a daily

---

1 Dictionary.com, s.v. "joy," www.dictionary.com/browse/joy; s.v. "entertainment," www.dictionary.com/browse/entertainment.

basis, do I act like I believe it? I usually settle for a Starbucks run and a scroll through Facebook rather than time with Jesus. Why? Well, maybe if I didn't believe the lie that these shallow pursuits can satisfy me, I wouldn't keep exchanging them for Jesus.

How is it that we keep getting surprised when this world and everything we are attracted to in it does not satisfy us? Our joy, or our lack of it, is a direct result of where we most spend our time and thoughts and energy. Your soul is most fulfilled in the small, quiet moments on the bedroom floor where you pray or in the comfy chair where you read your Bible or in your car where you worship God with singing. Your soul is more fulfilled by giving of yourself than by consuming.

Today Jesus is calling you to a backward way of discovering true joy—a way that will actually give you everything you're hoping for. In spending time with Jesus, you can allow your wild soul to be still. When resting in Him, you can remember that you are part of His incredible story. When delighting in Him, you will feel secure in your identity. And by listening to His voice, you will recognize the lies that promise fulfillment but fail to deliver, and instead find the truth that always delivers.

MEDITATE:
In your presence there is fullness of joy; at your right hand are pleasures forevermore. (Psalm 16:11)

REWIRE THE SPIRAL:
I can choose true joy over distraction.

God, I want to know joy in Your presence. When my impulse is to settle for being entertained and distracted, help me choose time with You and the satisfaction only You can bring. Amen.

SATISFIED

NOT LONG AGO, I TURNED OFF MY PHONE AND WENT OFFLINE, PLANning to stay away from screens for twenty-four hours. At first it felt freeing to have nothing vying for my attention. But it wasn't even an hour before I noticed myself reaching for my phone—like an addiction. Thankfully, each time I corrected myself and set my phone back down, I experienced an overwhelming sense of God's peace. My mind felt clearer. I was able to think, *You know what? I get to be present. I get to enjoy this day and the wonder of just being still with Jesus.* No Instagramming, no brilliant observations. Just Jesus and me and time. My soul filled up, and my view of life moved from the duty and responsibility I usually feel to the wonder of seeing even mundane moments from Jesus's perspective.

Let me tell you what happens when we learn to choose God over the distractions that vie for our thoughts and minds: He becomes so much better and dearer to us. And the apathy and numbness that lull us into a place where we crave entertainment and noise like a drug? It shifts. We wake up and crave God again. We discover the freedom that comes in choosing to put down the things we accidentally started to put our hope in.

I want to want God more. I want to reach for Him and enjoy His love for me rather than trying to get it from people or things that can never satisfy me. I don't want to search for a miraculous answer to the ache I can't shake, because I already have it. We already have Him.

Jesus is real and alive and with you right now, and He is the one who with His Word pours extravagant, rich, and unending floods of wonder into the voids of your soul. From Him flows everything you crave. Do you believe it? What's more, do you accept *Him* as enough?

Now let's be real. You are going to ache for what you don't have, and you are going to groan for more. Scripture says this is true, especially for those of us who have gotten a taste of God. We won't ever be completely, everlastingly full until we are home in the place we were made for—in heaven with God, at the marriage supper of the Lamb (Revelation 19:6–9). Only then will all your senses be satisfied and all your cravings fulfilled.

Until then, you will experience emptiness and want. After all, none of us can make earth be heaven, no matter what we do. We were made for another world. But in the meantime, Jesus is offering you a taste of the ultimate fulfillment to come. May that taste compel you to draw daily nearer to the only One who will ever fill your soul.

He satisfies the longing soul, and the hungry soul he fills with good things. (Psalm 107:9)

REWIRE THE SPIRAL:
Only Jesus can truly satisfy my longing heart.

God, when my thoughts spiral into distraction, help me realize where I am putting my hope. I choose to enjoy today with You, the one who really satisfies. Amen.

DRAW NEAR

IN GALATIANS 5, PAUL DESCRIBES THE EFFECTS BOTH OF RETREATING from God's presence and of drawing near. When we draw near, when we walk by the Spirit, we will not be subject to the constant craving to gratify our fleshly desires—to spin out into distractions that will pull us down, down, down. But if we retreat from His presence, we walk by the flesh, and things start to unravel.

Paul goes on to list what those desires of the flesh are: "sexual immorality, impurity, sensuality, idolatry, sorcery, enmity, strife, jealousy, fits of anger, rivalries, dissensions, divisions, envy, drunkenness, orgies, and things like these" (Galatians 5:19–21).

A lot of those sound extreme, yes, but some are all too familiar in our spiraling minds.

Paul also gives us an opposing list—a list of things that grow from a walk with the Spirit: "love, joy, peace, patience, kindness, goodness, faithfulness, gentleness, self-control" (Galatians 5:22–23). I don't know about you, but I could definitely use more of these in my heart and mind!

Now, comparing the two, it's easy to look at that litany of the works of the flesh and give ourselves a broad-brush pass. Since I don't tend to be tempted by sorcery or drunken orgies, I let myself off the hook regarding my own works of the flesh: my beloved Netflix, the fits of anger my kids seem to provoke in me, and the division I allow between God and me.

But, oh, how much I need His presence.

I need it daily, hourly, minute by minute. And so do you.

Why? Because even my best day pales in comparison with the reality He says I can live in when abiding by that last list. And the same goes for you.

He says we can become people who *love*—not just anecdotally but *impulsively,* as a reflexive act.

He says we can be *joyous* people. We can be people of kindness and patience and peace.

He says we can be *good.* Not to get some cosmic check mark but simply because our Father is good.

He says we can be *faithful. We don't have to waver in our faith.*

He says we can be *gentle* and *self-controlled.*

But if you and I are to live this way not just as a possibility but as an everyday, every-moment reality, we need to walk by the Spirit, instead of being jerked around by our swirling, chaotic thoughts. In other words, we urgently need time in the presence of God. And as you draw near to Him—day by day, hour by hour, and minute by minute—He will plant His fruit in you, and you will begin to flourish.

I say, walk by the Spirit, and you will not gratify the desires of the flesh. For the desires of the flesh are against the Spirit, and the desires of the Spirit are against the flesh. (Galatians 5:16–17)

I flourish when I draw near to God.

Father, help me to desire You—to long for You and Your presence and to recognize when I am pulling away. Amen.

THE RHYTHM OF REST

HAVE YOU HEARD A SYMPHONY LATELY? AT MY FIRST SYMPHONY PERformance, I honestly didn't expect to be impressed. In fact, I expected to be bored. Even when the notes from a violin cut through the air in a stunning solo, I wasn't moved. Then the flutes joined, and I let down my guard a little. Then every one of the nearly one hundred instruments flooded the room, and I fell apart. I leaned back and tried to process it, but comprehension was almost impossible. Each string, key, note, and rest working in unison built a beauty I didn't even know existed.

In the same way, you and I were built to enjoy the symphony God is always playing. We might hear only a single seemingly random cymbal crash or a bellowing undertone of a cello in our mundane days. We might overlook the moment of silence between the notes, not knowing that pause gives the music its structure. We might miss the whole harmony because the parts are all broken up and have lost their beauty. Yet all our days—the boring, the exciting, the busy, and the quiet—make up our song. God's stunning symphony.

When I take the time to listen to God's symphony, I start to feel like an absolute fool for spending even one day of my gift of life here numb, checked out, distracted, or fiddling away on my own instead of looking to the Conductor up there on the podium.

But it's so easy to do.

Because we forget the bigger symphony, the great and hidden story, we start to resent and even neglect the small, mundane parts of our lives. We choose distraction instead. But if we could realize the small parts are building heaven, maybe we wouldn't check out from them. If we could recognize Jesus in the middle of each ordinary, messy, mundane moment, maybe we wouldn't take them for granted. Because He is in every moment. He's in every effort we make to look to Him, as well as in the moments when we forget to do so. We might meet with Him in our cubicles, in the carpool lanes, at the table, and even at the kitchen sink. These are the places where we dwell with Him.

Vision and rest, work and joy, and Jesus and difficulty are meant to coexist. When you get caught up in your own spirals of striving and distraction, you lose sight of the beauty of the grand symphony unfolding. As you draw near to Him, though, you can hear it. He's making something beautiful with your life.

MEDITATE:

Call to me and I will answer you, and will tell you great and hidden things that you have not known. (Jeremiah 33:3)

REWIRE THE SPIRAL:

I can hear God's glory in the quiet moments of every day.

Lord, in the small, silent, everyday moments today, open my heart to the symphony You are creating. I choose to call to You and listen for Your bigger song. Amen.

DAY

34

FRESH START

THE CLOSER I GET TO GOD, THE MORE FASCINATED I BECOME BY THE intricate design of our bodies and minds. And all my research has confirmed again and again what the Bible says to be true. For instance, we now know that each thought you think matters a *lot*. Scientifically speaking, every thought we think *changes our brains*.

Here's some science for you: Inside your brain are about 86 billion nerve cells, called *neurons*.[1] They mean *everything* to how we process life. Inside the neurons are *microtubules*, which have been called "the brains of the cell." They're a little like a Lego set, building and rebuilding.[2] Inside your neurons, those microtubules are constantly building and taking apart and adjusting and shifting and stopping and starting again, in accordance with—you guessed it!—*your every thought*.[3] With each thought you think, those microtubules work hard to provide mental scaffolding

---

1 James Randerson, "How Many Neurons Make a Human Brain? Billions Fewer Than We Thought," *Guardian,* February 28, 2012, www.theguardian.com/science/blog/2012/feb/28/how-many-neurons-human-brain.

2 Jon Lieff, "Are Microtubules the Brain of the Neuron?," Searching for the Mind, November 29, 2015, http://jonlieffmd.com/blog/are-microtubules-the-brain-of-the-neuron.

3 Lieff, "Are Microtubules?"

to support that thought. That scaffolding gives structure to the entire nerve cell and physically alters your brain.

And how long does it take for a microtubule to finish the scaffolding? From creation to completion: Ten. Minutes.

From the time you think a thought to that thought having physiologically *changed your brain,* ten minutes have passed.[4] Your one thought has awakened some neurons and allowed others to drift to sleep. It has built an entire city in some parts of your mind and left others a total ghost town.

All from one simple thought.

There are two ways to look at this. One is frightening: *If I think even one negative thought, I could wreck my whole brain in ten minutes flat!* But on the flip side, if you have made a habit of thinking negative thoughts, you're only ten minutes away from a fresh start.

With each positive choice made, we are training ourselves to cultivate the mind of Christ. It's like cutting a road in the woods. At first the path is just flattened leaves. But over time the demand for that path will cause someone to lay gravel, and then pour cement, and then put in streetlights. Eventually the path is so clear that it would be senseless to take another route.

Training yourself to "take a good path" in your thinking is crucial, because when you're stressed out or hurting, you'll head for the default road you've built. But be encouraged: God gives you a choice to make a fresh start as many times as you need to.

---

4 John McCrone, quoted in Dawson Church, *The Genie in Your Genes: Epigenetic Medicine and the New Biology of Intention* (Santa Rosa, CA: Elite Books, 2007), 141.

MEDITATE:
Put on the new self, which is being renewed in knowledge after the image of its creator. (Colossians 3:10)

REWIRE THE SPIRAL:
God continues to give me fresh starts.

Father, thank You for the way You constructed my mind. Thank You for making me renewable, rebuildable, and changeable in Your image. Lead me to choose a good path today. Amen.

EMOTION

Hurt

THOUGHT

People are not trustworthy,
and life will not work out

BEHAVIOR

Critical of self and others

RELATIONSHIPS

Sarcastic and cold

CONSEQUENCE

Cynical

CONSEQUENCE

Trusting

RELATIONSHIPS

Engaged and curious

BEHAVIOR

Believes the best in others

THOUGHT

God is trustworthy and will,
in the end, work all things out

I choose to delight ⟶

EMOTION

Hurt

FROM
CYNICISM
TO
DELIGHT

UNVEILED

DO YOU GET ANNOYED WHEN PEOPLE ARE OPTIMISTIC? WHEN SOME-one is nice, do you wonder what that person wants? When things are going well, are you waiting for the bottom to fall out? Do you quickly notice people's flaws? Do you feel misunderstood or worry about getting taken advantage of? Are you guarded when you meet someone new? Do you wonder why people can't get it together? Are you often sarcastic? If any of these ring true, cynicism may have invaded your headspace.

Similar to a virus, cynicism destroys our relationships and our ability to delight in the world around us and fully engage with others. Cynicism says, "I'm surrounded by incompetence, fraudsters, and disappointment." The lie of cynicism is, *People are not trustworthy, and life will not work out.* The truth is, *God is trustworthy and will, in the end, work all things together for good.* God always has an abundance of joy and delight for us, but we'll miss it with our arms crossed when we're stuck in cynicism.

What's the opposite of cynicism? Awe. Researchers found an interesting connection when studying awe and beauty: When we experience awe, we move toward others in beneficial ways. When overcome by the grandeur of a snowy mountain peak or delighted by a beautiful song, when sitting silently in an old church and marveling at the way the sunlight seeps through the stained-glass windows, or when delighted by our children's squeals as they run through the sprinkler, we let go of our "it's all about me" fixation. We are freed from being the center of our own worlds for just a moment, and in doing so, we become more invested in the well-being of others. We're more generous and less entitled.[1]

In other words, **delight tears down our walls and allows hope and worship to flood in. When cynicism spirals, we can choose to delight in God and see signs of His work in the world around us.** And guess how worship springs up in us? When we look for delight instead of problems.

Today's meditation verse is Paul's description of what happens when we, like the Israelites, turn our gazes away from the things that fade and look in delight to the eternal God. It's like a veil is removed, and we're transformed: God works in us and makes our lives brighter and more beautiful.

MEDITATE:
We all, with unveiled face, beholding the glory of the Lord, are being transformed into the same image from one degree of glory to another.
(2 Corinthians 3:18)

REWIRE THE SPIRAL:
I can choose delight over the spirals of cynicism.

God, when I get jaded about things going on in my life, help me see that there's another choice. Open my eyes and heart to wonder and delight today. Amen.

1   Paul K. Piff et al., "Awe, the Small Self, and Prosocial Behavior," *Journal of Personality and Social Psychology* 108, no. 6 (2015): 883, www.apa.org/pubs/journals/releases/psp-pspi0000018.pdf.

CHOOSE WHAT YOU SEE

IF WE WENT TOGETHER TO A PARTY ONE EVENING AND THE PEOPLE WE sat next to were complaining about the tasteless food, the lame playlist, and the rude hosts, we'd come away with the impression that the party had been a bad experience. Truth be told, we might not have minded the food or the environment, but those gripes would sway us to that negative side.

We would walk away thinking, *That was a terrible party.*

But if we went to the same party and instead sat next to people who were raving about the delicious food, the energetic music, the thoughtful seating, and the kind and generous hosts, we would leave saying, "What a fun party!"

What if instead of a party, we were talking about our lives? What if we are *choosing* to be unhappy? Rather than seeing the best and celebrating the good, how often have we chosen to see only the struggles and complain about the bad?

We often have the legitimate worry that if we choose to see the best in life, we're going to get taken advantage of. Maybe if we don't keep our guard up, people might see our naivete and target us. That's fair.

But when we live guarded, we become consumed by self-preservation, self-protection, and debilitating pessimism. Who wants to live that way?

It's true that cynicism has become esteemed in our culture, as if we've concluded the cynics know something the rest of us don't. They are prepared, guarded, and *aware* at a level the rest of us are too flighty to grasp. But at its core, cynicism is *always* driven by fear of the future or by anger toward the past. Either we're afraid of something that might not ever occur or we project something that *has* occurred onto all the days that are to come. We buy into the lie that it's too risky to hope for good things.

But is it really? The enemy's strategy is to flood our thoughts with visions of all that is wrong in this broken, fallen world to the point we don't even think to look for the positive anymore. Cynicism just becomes the way we think, and we don't even notice what it's doing to us.

I think it's time we notice. Otherwise, we not only miss out on a pretty good party but we also miss out on the wonder that surrounds us—on celebrating the good things God wants to bless us with.

What could transform in your life today if you chose to see the best?

MEDITATE:
This is the day that the LORD has made; let us rejoice and be glad in it. (Psalm 118:24)

REWIRE THE SPIRAL:
It's never too risky for me to choose hope.

God, *You make it possible for me to hope for good things. When the world's current of cynicism threatens to suck me under, remind me that I don't have to go with it. Amen.*

DAY

37

MIND-BLOWING BEAUTY

HOW DO YOU FEEL WHEN YOU LOOK AT SOMETHING TRULY BEAUTIFUL?
Do you get goosebumps? Are you tearful? Overwhelmed? Elated? Beauty
interrupts us, awakens us, undoes us, cuts us open, and restarts our
hearts. Beauty is God's evidence of something far more wonderful coming, a world beyond the one we can imagine, even in the most spectacu-
lar moments here. Beauty is proof of a God better than what we hope for.
A God who blows our minds. And a God who designed us.

God has gone to great lengths to craft each individual leaf on a ma-
jestic tree, every crevasse in a sublime mountain. Hasn't He applied even
greater intention and care to our lives? We aren't mistakes. We aren't acci-
dents. Our situations aren't hidden from God. He's crafted us all so care-
fully and so creatively, and He has applied His creativity to our world.

Think of *peacocks,* for crying out loud. The colors and detail are so
unnecessarily delightful. Who but God would do that? Or imagine the
way a symphony swells to something we can barely take in. My coun-
tenance and posture lift whenever I hear something like that. Or think
of the patterns of a flower's petals—three for lilies, five for buttercups,

twenty-one for chicory, thirty-four for daisies. That doesn't just *happen,* you know? God thought of them and whipped them out.

Picture the perfect spirals both of hurricanes and of seashells. Or the structured flight patterns of birds. Or the design of our elbows and fingers and toes. It's everywhere you look, if you only have eyes to see. There is such intention. Such craftsmanship. Such incredible functionality. Such beauty. Such *proof.*

Scientists wonder whether it's all mere coincidence. We know better. Goodness is meant not merely to make us feel good but to point us to God.

At these encounters with things that are excellent, that are lovely, that are true, we come away different from how we were before. We come away totally changed. We are changed for the better when we train our attention on that which is beautiful, on that which is authentic and compelling and good. Beyond the positive emotional experience they spark in us, those good things can transform the soul.

Cynicism crumbles in the presence of beauty.

When we choose to see beauty, we choose delight.

MEDITATE:
How great are your works,
O LORD! (Psalm 92:5)

REWIRE THE SPIRAL:
Beauty surrounds me, and
I choose to see it.

God, Your creativity and care are astounding. Thank You for making me and every beautiful thing on this earth with such breathtaking care. Open my eyes today to see and experience Your delight. Amen.

BREAKING DOWN OUR WALLS

MRIs OF THE BRAIN SHOW THAT WHEN WE ARE IN AWE OF SOMETHING, we become less self-centered, more others-centered, and more aware of the world and those around us.[1] In other words, feelings of awe shut down selfishness.

We worship when we experience awe.

And cynicism and worship cannot coexist.

I think about how cynical I've been at times, about how my arms-folded self just *wasn't* going to choose to trust. I didn't *want* someone coming to help me—which is, of course, the problem. Cynicism is especially powerful as a tool in Satan's hands, because when you and I are struck by it, we don't see our need to be helped.

We think we're just fine, thank you very much.

The truth? We desperately need Jesus.

Bruno Mars released a love song years ago that says, "I'd catch a

1   Avery Foley, "Wired for Awe," Answers in Genesis, March 1, 2018, https://answersingenesis.org/human-body/brain/wired-awe.

grenade for ya . . . jump in front of a train for ya."[2] While it was a catchy tune, I don't think Bruno would really do that for ya, you know?

But guess who would?

Guess who did?

Jesus, Son of God. He faced the greatest sacrifice to bust through our cool "I don't need anybody" attitude, our intellect and shame and doubt. He entered our reality and arrested us with the story we longed to be true.

I picture His face with a look of outright determination, of commitment and concern, of "I'm comin' for you!" confidence. And, friend, this is what I picture for you when I think of you out there fighting all kinds of darkness and spiraling out.

Jesus came for us—for you and me, even when our arms were crossed. He still came for bitter, cranky, unsure, doubting, cynical, negative us.

If the interrupting thought that shifts all the others is *I have a choice,* there is one reason that is true. It's because Jesus first chose us.

It's because He busted down the door and rescued us in His beauty and kindness. He suited up and came for us. And that is why we shouldn't wallow in cynicism, expecting the worst.

Because we have been promised a forever better than we can imagine.

---

2   Bruno Mars et al., "Grenade," *Doo-Wops & Hooligans,* copyright © 2010, Elektra Entertainment Group.

MEDITATE:

Neither death nor life, nor angels nor rulers, nor things present nor things to come, nor powers, nor height nor depth, nor anything else in all creation, will be able to separate us from the love of God in Christ Jesus our Lord. (Romans 8:38–39)

REWIRE THE SPIRAL:

I have a choice, because Jesus chose me.

Jesus, thank You for coming for me. Thank You for choosing me. Thank You for filling me with hope and for making it possible for me to choose worship today. Amen.

BEAUTY OVER BITTERNESS

A CYNIC IS SOMEONE WHO "SHOWS A DISPOSITION TO DISBELIEVE IN the sincerity or goodness of human motives and actions."[1] If you're like me, the disbelief and suspicion hardly stops there. Eventually we begin to distrust God too.

Cynicism erodes our ability to see God rightly.

Cynicism at its root is a refusal to believe that God is in control and God is good. Cynicism is interpreting the world and God based on hurt you've experienced and the wounds that still lie gaping open. It forces you to look horizontally at people rather than vertically to God.

Sometimes it's hard to see that the hurt we've experienced is absolutely driving our behavior.

The truth is, cynicism usually grows because we think we deserve better than we are getting. At the root of cynicism is crippling hurt. Cynicism says that nobody can be trusted, and that we're never, ever safe.

---

1   Oxford English Dictionary Online, s.v. "cynic," www.oed.com.

At my most cynical, I felt as if I had fallen into a crack and God either hadn't noticed or hadn't cared enough to rescue me. I caught myself thinking things like, *Why would He abandon me to plans I didn't create and didn't want without consulting me? Why did He let me slip into a dark crack and leave me there? It figures.*

My fear gave way to a protective shell of cynicism that blocked not only the potential for hurt but also the potential for joy. Yes, I had been faithful to evict certain gloom-and-doom thoughts from my mind, but unless I helped better thinking move in and settle down, I'd keep trapping myself in terrible thoughts.

But then God used, of all things, a piece of art to get to me. It was beautiful, and it disarmed me. Beauty cracked me open.

Those things Paul said to think about—all things beautiful and excellent and just—they are what can soften a cynical heart and bring sanity to a chaotic mind.

God uses beauty to unlock our tightly crossed arms.

Beauty is evidence of something beyond ourselves. Beauty is evidence of a world yet to come. Beauty is evidence of a Creator who is loving and profoundly delightful. Beauty floods in and interrupts when, instead of cynicism, we choose trust.

Finally, brothers, whatever is true, whatever is honorable, whatever is just, whatever is pure, whatever is lovely, whatever is commendable, if there is any excellence, if there is anything worthy of praise, think about these things. **(Philippians 4:8)**

Beauty is evidence that God loves me and delights in me.

Holy Spirit, please show me where any hurts in my life have allowed cynicism to creep in. Let me be ministered to by Your beauty and healed with the love and power behind it. Amen.

DAY

40

THE HOPEFUL ADVOCATE

CONSTANTLY THROUGHOUT SCRIPTURE, WE ARE TOLD TO BE SOBER AND discerning. That's not the same as being cynical. Cynicism is a mindset that brings us down, but we *should* be wise and discerning and judge rightly about the world by speaking and acting against the wrong we see in it. I hope that people would see followers of Jesus not as cynical critics of the world but as hopeful advocates—especially in cases of injustice.

So we should advocate loudly when injustice occurs—for righteous causes. It's not that we should never speak out about injustice or ignore the evil in the world. We should. The danger is when we're overcome by the evil we see or motivated to act solely out of our own hurt. Instead, we should be driven to act out of obedience and out of hope that God alone can bring change.

I believe for my African American son that a world could exist that's better than the one we're in now. It's not that I don't soberly see where we are today. The key is constantly moving forward and praying, *God, redeem what is broken, heal what is hurting, and bring hope where there is hopelessness.* It's a productive moving forward. That's what God's called us to do.

He has called us and created us to be overcomers and reconcilers. Not passive judgment givers. And I think that's where cynicism gets us. It puts us on the sidelines of what's happening in the world, and in other people's lives, and convinces us to cross our arms. And rather than working toward action, we start judging motives that may or may not even be true. God constantly says, *Don't judge motives. I'm the only judge of motives* (1 Corinthians 4:5). We can barely judge our own motives, for Pete's sake. So for us to assume the worst about people when we don't even know them is not helpful. I'd rather move toward action where there's darkness. That's who I want to be. Not someone who is paralyzed with cynicism and doubt about everybody being evil, but someone who believes, "You know what? We can accomplish a lot of good together because of God."

MEDITATE:
I am sending you out as sheep in the midst of wolves, so be wise as serpents and innocent as doves. (Matthew 10:16)

REWIRE THE SPIRAL:
God's hope makes good change possible.

Father, please make me both wise and innocent, a hopeful advocate for justice in this life. I choose not to let cynicism sideline me in a world where there is so much good to be done. Amen.

IMPERFECT CHURCH

I DON'T KNOW WHAT YOUR RELATIONSHIP WITH CHURCH IS. IT MAY BE your happy place—where you go to get nourished and share God's love. It may be a source of deep trauma for you, and you can't even step through the door. Or maybe after years of seeing brokenness in the church, you've decided it's not to be trusted. But hear me out: At its best, church is a place where health and wholeness spread—where we are imperfect and even broken but shaped by the mind of Christ. It's where our minds can be changed for the better.

When you think about how *contagious* our minds are, and about how, when we're conformed to the mind of Christ, we can influence everyone around us for powerful, almost indescribable good, church becomes a place of hope. It's a place where we pass that hope and health around to each other.

Recently, my friend Jess sent me a text with a picture of her dad. He is a godly man, a great dad, and a faithful husband. He also is a man with a substance abuse problem.

He finished a season in rehab a few months ago, and he returned to his church and community on a *mission.* After his program finished, he went back and began leading Bible studies at the rehab facility he'd just left.

The picture Jess texted me was of six men with different ages, ethnicities, and interests. They were all smiles, seated around a dinner table. Jess wrote, "My dad woke up Saturday morning with the idea to invite his rehab buddies over for dinner, so he and my mom made the invite, and a few hours later they all showed up. My family is still fragile, but these are the things that help me see that God really does bring beauty from ashes."

This to me is the beauty of an imperfect church. Only God can take our most broken parts and turn them into moments of hope around grilled hamburgers and potato salad. Only God can take the thing we want to hide and build the greatest story we will ever tell. Only God can turn people we might have looked down on into friends and co-laborers and brothers in Him.

Only God.

When I think of the church God has built on this earth, I think of the place where this kind of healing happens. What could happen in the church if, instead of treating the body of Christ with cynicism for its brokenness, we went in with contagious humility? If we let God turn us into family in the way only He can?

MEDITATE:

Let us consider how to stir up one another to love and good works, not neglecting to meet together, as is the habit of some, but encouraging one another. (Hebrews 10:24–25)

REWIRE THE SPIRAL:

God offers healing to His imperfect family.

Father, thank You for the way You've made Your people to function as one body. Please help me fight against cynicism and for humility and hope in the context of Your church. Amen.

BE LIFE GIVING

WHY IS WHAT WE BELIEVE IMPORTANT? BECAUSE WE RISE TO WHAT WE believe. I see this in my kids all the time.

When I speak life-giving truth to my son Cooper, he will rise to that. I recently said to him before school, "Buddy, you're a leader. Act like one today." He came home later telling me what a great day he'd had, all because he believed this about himself. He rose to that compliment. He rose to what I saw in him. In the same way, we've got to realize that how we think influences what we say and what we believe about ourselves and the people around us.

This is how much I believe this is true. I had a friend recently who didn't know if she was pregnant with a boy or a girl, and she said, "I just don't think I'll be a good mom if it's a girl." And I had to say, "Hey, friend. Stop. Don't speak that. Don't say that. Don't speak negatively over your unborn child. Don't engage in that toxic stuff. Don't even think it." She's so much better than she gives herself credit for.

Some of us have spoken and thought negatively and cynically about ourselves for way too long, but we can shift that today. We don't have to speak it. We don't have to think it. Because the place of interruption is not in our words. The key is to control our thoughts. We don't need to give cynical thoughts energy, because our kids are picking up on it, our friends are picking up on it, and the people we are mentoring and leading and discipling are all picking up on it. If we can start to speak life over ourselves and others instead, we can be life giving. The opposite of cynical. We can be life giving, life speaking, and life thinking, for ourselves and others. It's a different way to live, and the world is aching for it.

When you live this way, yes, some people will think you're naive, but most people will just want to hear from you and be around you, because they need people who will not only speak truth but actually believe truth for them. Today make the choice to be life giving to yourself and to others around you. Let your mouth speak from the abundance of goodness in your heart and mind. Because you can choose better thoughts—and rise to them.

MEDITATE:
Out of the abundance of the heart the mouth speaks.
(Matthew 12:34)

REWIRE THE SPIRAL:
I will give my energy to what gives life.

Jesus, please help me set a higher bar with my thoughts today. Thank You that You made me with the ability to choose what lives in my mind and heart, and what doesn't.

A SLOW LEAK

HAVE YOU EVER FELT A SLOW LEAK IN YOUR LIFE? IT'S LIKE WITH MY tire. Every time I get in the car, the air in the tire goes down, but it will take weeks to get to where it's a dangerous level. This leak is extra slow, but the car keeps alerting me that it's getting lower and lower. That's exactly what cynicism is. It's a slow leak of joy in our lives. Because if we fixate on the negative, we are not ever going to be happy.

As Christians, we have a lot of bigger goals than happiness, right? Happiness is not our ultimate goal. But at the end of the day, what we think about—and the joy that inhabits our minds and our hearts—should be of great concern in Christianity. Who wants to follow after people who are following after God if they don't have any joy? Nobody, really. We have a God who issues ultimate joy, ultimate hope, and ultimate peace—peace that surpasses understanding. Philippians 4:7 tells us so. Shouldn't we be reflecting those things if we actually believe we've been given them and if we're actually following God?

Yet cynicism makes us question all our authorities so we never submit. It makes us question all our institutions so we never participate. It makes us question all our friendships so we never connect. It makes us question our family members so we never, ever feel safe. It erodes our confidence and our joy. It diminishes all the gifts that God has given us to help us follow Him, to help us grow up in the faith, and to help us live out full, abundant, and obedient lives.

So how do we change this? Well, for one, we've got to be careful about what we're feeding our souls.

For example, candidly, I had to get off Twitter. It was a social media influence in my life that always made me cynical. How could I believe the best when it seemed like a constant input in my life was full of angry people believing the worst?

We must guard all our inputs, even the people and voices in our lives. I'm talking about the people who are going to be in our ear every day, who are truly close to us. We all need to choose people who are life giving and who see the good in the world and in us. And we too can be people who fill others up. Who keep each other going. We can stop the slow leak of joy by choosing to ignore cynical influences and choosing to experience wonder and joy instead.

MEDITATE:
The joy of the LORD is your strength. (Nehemiah 8:10)

REWIRE THE SPIRAL:
I can protect my joy by guarding my inputs.

Father, please reveal to me where my joy may be leaking, and lead me to make the choices I need to stop that leak. Amen.

DAY

44

TIP THE SCALE

IS THERE ANYTHING IN YOUR LIFE THAT IS TIPPING YOU TOWARD CYNI-cism? That is not leading to life and peace?

It's critical to spot what could be causing a cynical spirit in you toward people. It could be other people: gossipy neighbors, negative family members, or friends that are always complaining about their spouses or jobs or co-workers. I'm not saying you should never spend time with them, but you should guard your mind by not spending *all* your time with them. And when you're with them, have a plan of defense.

Gossip happens. But how do we turn the conversation? How do we bring life and peace into it? We can develop a collection of sound bites that turn the conversation around. "So what's going good with you lately?" "Well, I like her." Anything to inject something positive. We've got to be light in dark places, but we also need people and places that are full of light and that bring energy, life, and joy into us. We need to make choices that break the cynicism spiral and tip us back toward joy.

People can bring light, and beauty can bring light to our hearts. A song can do that. A beautiful play. A poem. A painting. A scene in God's creation. It pierces you. It just takes you out. It touches something in you that common sense, reasonableness, and truth can sometimes miss. Again, beauty is evidence that there's a Creator who is loving and profoundly delightful.

The delight and power of God is expressed to us daily through creation, through animals, and through adorable little babies. I think these are the things that God uses to say to us, *I'm safe, I'm trustworthy, I'm likable, and My world is good.* And yes, there is sin around us—in institutions sometimes and, yes, in people. What cynicism says is that sin should make us never trust people. Delight says there is goodness and trustworthiness too. And redemption and joy. Some days people and situations will disappoint us. But I would rather live full of joy, believing the good and getting burned every once in a while, than constantly wait to get burned while only seeing the negative. That is a sad way to live.

So keep believing good for our country, for your church, for your family. Keep believing good for this generation. You can choose to tip the scale and believe good.

Keep your heart with all vigilance, for from it flow the springs of life. **(Proverbs 4:23)**

I can choose to believe the best in others.

God, no matter what happens in the world, please help me see the good around me. I choose to have hope. Amen.

NEW MERCIES

ONE OF MY VERY FAVORITE PASSAGES IN SCRIPTURE IS THE ONE THAT says God's mercies are new every morning (Lamentations 3:23). Every morning I say it to myself. Every time I've had a good cry or gotten in a good fight, when I wake up the next day, I will say it over myself. His mercies are new *every* morning. It is like a good cold shower. It is a reminder and refreshment that we get a new day. The sun is up, we're still breathing, and God still loves us. And we have grace to move and make mistakes and be imperfect.

We all need this mercy just as much as we need correction and improvement. We get to the health and the freedom we're craving this backward way, not by shoving to-dos down our throats but by gently being led to water. It's what Jesus does for us. In Psalm 23, we see this gentle leading of the Spirit: *I will take you and lead you by still water.* I love that side of God. It is why we can call Him a Friend and a loving Father, because He has not reprimanded us. He refreshes us.

I hope that as you continue through this journey to stop your spirals, you can see how God is leading you to still waters. That you would feel a storyline building of hope and of help. Because I believe both things are readily available to us. We will not necessarily feel fixed at some magical point in the future. I've seen for too long that the same struggles I had at ten years old are the struggles I still have today. Now, that doesn't mean I'm defined by those struggles. It just means they rear their heads because of my story, my proclivities, and my personality.

Everything I've always struggled with is still what I struggle with today. But over time, their power over me has weakened. We do have spiritual authority and power in our lives. But we also have a gentle, compassionate God who leads us by still waters and whose mercies endlessly renew.

Today my hope is that, yes, you would know that you are more than a conqueror because of Jesus Christ, and that you do have power over your thoughts. Stand by that. However, you also have a very compassionate God who cries with you and asks you to do the same. Today you're still in the war. You're still in the mess. So ultimately I hope you feel mercy, new every morning, no matter the struggles. God loves you. He's with you. He's for you. And He's helping you.

MEDITATE:
The steadfast love of the LORD never ceases; his mercies never come to an end; they are new every morning. (Lamentations 3:22–23)

REWIRE THE SPIRAL:
God's mercy is new for me every morning.

Jesus, thank You for Your constant mercy. Thank You for leading me to still waters and restoring my soul. Keep me returning again and again to You. Amen.

EMOTION
Anger

CONSEQUENCE
Selflessly serves others

THOUGHT
I am better than other people

RELATIONSHIPS
Generous and joyful

BEHAVIOR
Self-promoter and self-protector

BEHAVIOR
Promotes and protects others

RELATIONSHIPS
Draining and neglected

THOUGHT
The more I choose God and others over myself, the more joyful I will be

I choose to serve God + others over myself ⟶

CONSEQUENCE
Unknown and feeling unloved

EMOTION
Anger

FROM SELF-IMPORTANCE TO HUMILITY

THE WEAPON OF HUMILITY

WE ALL LIKE A LITTLE BOOST TO OUR SELF-ESTEEM NOW AND AGAIN. Yet, as much as we crave affirmation, is our own self-esteem a valid guide for navigating life? Our swirling thoughts tell us, *Not so much.*

So often in our search for confidence or self-esteem, we compare and contrast, justify and judge, and spend a ridiculous amount of time contemplating our identity and place in this world. This is why the apostle Paul cautioned us not to think of ourselves more highly than we ought but to honor one another instead (Romans 12:3, 10).

But living this way requires us to deliberately and repeatedly interrupt the natural trajectory of our thoughts. We need a powerful weapon for shifting out of harmful patterns of thinking, and the one that shifts us out of getting stuck in our own selves is *humility.*

One of the enemies of our minds specifically rampant in this generation is the inflated view of self being handed to us all over social media, in the shows and movies we watch, and even in the self-help books we read. We're fed a continuous message of how much we matter and how very important we are—and we believe every word of the deceiver. And, thanks to technology, we live in a world where everybody can be somewhat important. We all get a microphone. We all can start a YouTube channel or be known on Instagram. Self-importance sneaks up on us, because it is easy to self-inflate these days. We can make ourselves a big deal, even if it's to a small audience, all day long. The enemy dangles the temptation of self-importance right in front of our faces, every minute of every day. So, for the good of our own minds, we've got to identify that temptation and figure out how to fight it.

We have to make a different choice.

So when the enemy invites you to taste the fruit of self-importance, you can choose instead to take up your cross and follow Jesus, knowing that your identity is anchored in Him alone. The lie is, *If I could only feel better about myself, or become more important, I would be happy.* The upside-down truth is, *The more I choose God and others over myself, the more joyful I will be.* The truth is, finding significance in ourselves just never feels as good as we think it will.

MEDITATE:
By the grace given to me I say to everyone among you not to think of himself more highly than he ought to think. . . . Love one another with brotherly affection. Outdo one another in showing honor. (Romans 12:3, 10)

REWIRE THE SPIRAL:
I can choose humility over getting stuck in myself.

God, with Your Spirit, please reveal in me anywhere I am spiraling into myself. Help me recognize the tendency in and around me, so I can choose to look upward and outward. Amen.

CHOOSE LIKE JESUS

SAY I REACT UNFAIRLY TO A FRIEND ONE DAY, AND THEN I FEEL ANGSTY and guilty and mad. To make myself feel better, I stuff down those feelings and just move on. Later I feel guilty again, but instead of apologizing, I start listing the reasons I was right and she was wrong. A puffed-up pride fills my senses and causes me to keep justifying, defending, abdicating responsibility, and refusing to budge. I am the centerpiece in this little scenario, which has fractured the tie between my friend and me.

Notice any trends in that sequence?

I, I, I, I, I.

When our thoughts are consumed with ourselves, we forget how very much we need Jesus. We buy the lie of self-empowerment: *You've got this.* We forget that we are called to take up our cross and follow Him, to share in His sufferings, and to be humble and gentle and kind.[1]

Humility. It just feels so *difficult* sometimes, you know? I am no

---

1 Matthew 16:24; 1 Peter 4:13; Ephesians 4:1–3, NIV.

better than a toddler who would rather lose all his favorite things than say, "I'm sorry. I was wrong."

Then I remember Jesus.

Guiltless and wrongfully accused.

Yet still completely humble of heart.

Our friend the apostle Paul pointed to Jesus as our guide for how to let go of greatness. He wrote, "In your relationships with one another, have the same mindset as Christ Jesus" (Philippians 2:5, NIV).

And what was that mindset?

He emptied Himself by taking the form of a servant. He humbled Himself by becoming obedient to death. Does this sound as convicting to you as it does to me?

Jesus's sacrifice wasn't merely a kind act from Jesus for humankind. It was also intended to be an example—as in, a move that *His followers would consistently make.* Inviting the death of self-centeredness. Enduring the death of dreams. Allowing for the death of hyper-consumerism. Being *least awesome, least liked, last.*

Jesus humbled Himself so that we'd be compelled to live lives of deep humility too. That is, if we so *choose.* We can make a better choice than getting stuck in ourselves. We can say today, "I choose humility like Christ's."

MEDITATE:

Though he was in the form of God, [Jesus] did not count equality with God a thing to be grasped, but emptied himself, by taking the form of a servant, being born in the likeness of men. And being found in human form, he humbled himself by becoming obedient to the point of death, even death on a cross. (Philippians 2:6–8)

REWIRE THE SPIRAL:

I can choose the example of Jesus to go lower instead of higher.

Jesus, please show me what it means to truly live like You, in revolutionary humility. When my thoughts get consumed with myself, lead me to choose a better way. Amen.

REST IN GOD'S POWER

HUMILITY IS IMPOSSIBLY OPPOSITE THE WAYS OF THIS WORLD. OUR SPIN-ning thoughts can hardly comprehend being at rest instead of jockeying for approval.

Yet, interestingly enough, we weren't built to be the center of our own worlds.

Self-importance can mess with what's known as "mirror neurons" in our brains, which help us empathize with others, mirror their emotions and reactions, and connect on a visceral level. When we are puffed up with thoughts of how important we are, our mirror neurons are impaired. That's why, in our spiraling of self-importance, truly understanding other points of view seems nearly impossible. Instead of resting and connecting, we spin and spin.

The apostle Paul embodied the idea of being at rest, even when being blamed or despised. While imprisoned—most likely in a house-arrest situation—wondering whether he would be executed, he declared his central desire to rejoice, to praise God, and to spread the good news wherever he was. Paul possessed an incredible disregard for his losses and accomplishments alike. He disregarded the things that the rest of the world esteems. He even disregarded himself. He couldn't care less what happened to him, just as long as he could know Jesus better. In fact, all worldly gains and those things the rest of us count as important? He counted them as a loss, compared to Christ.

I find these insights from Paul staggering, especially in our day and age. If I had to name the most destructive line of thinking in our twenty-first-century culture, it would be our incessant quest to be great. We spend a lot of effort trying to become distinct, successful, smarter, stronger, thinner . . . greater. We love being great. It's so great to be so great.

Even followers of Jesus want to be great—as in, *accomplished and successful.* Sure, we may couch it in acceptable terms, like "doing great things for the kingdom" or "making God's name famous." But somehow our thoughts subtly become centered not on Him but on ourselves—how we can achieve our goals, realize our dreams, enlarge our influence, or position ourselves for success.

We spend a lot of time looking around at others—not so we can encourage them in their growth but so we can figure out how we measure up. We convince ourselves that God wants us to be amazing. We are all about empowerment. But lasting joy will come only when God is in the center. Not when you are empowered but when you rest in His power.

Whatever gain I had, I counted as loss for the sake of Christ. **(Philippians 3:7)**

God is better than anything this world offers.

God, thank You that I don't have to try to claw myself to greatness and that I can rest in You. When I become focused on accomplishment, help me expand my world beyond myself and look for what You are doing. Amen.

SEEKING SELF-IMPORTANCE

SELF-IMPORTANCE FEELS SO GOOD. AND THE SPIRAL IT TAKES US ON easily tricks us into thinking it's for the best, while subtly blocking us from true peace. Spirals like fear and anxiety don't feel so good. But the spiral of self-importance feels great. It feels wonderful to be important. It is deep in our bones to crave it, to want it, to fight for it, to live for it. We chase it in different ways, but ultimately it is the impulse to make ourselves seen, known, loved, and important. Whether it's through relationships, wealth, accomplishment, or fame—things we want to be or are disappointed that we're not—we seek to be important. It is an addiction, and a dangerous one. If we do not notice this in ourselves, in our ministries, or in our journey of following Jesus, some subtle things happen.

One of those subtle things is that we start to care a lot about how people view us. We constantly find ourselves thinking about it. We wonder whether people like us, notice us, like our posts, or support us. Our eyes dart back and forth, taking in what people are seeing about us. This pursuit is exhausting and draining, because largely, other people are not really going to notice us that much. And if they do, they're going to have a mixed bag of opinions, no matter how we're living. It's simply not achievable to be loved by everybody, because it's not under our control.

The real mind-bender is when we start to care about whether people think we're humble or not. We can look humble and build a story that tells the world we are humble, when our quest for humility is actually based on self-importance and pride. Ugh! So what do we do to break out of this vicious cycle?

The change we need is not necessarily about the decisions we make outwardly in life. It's about the posture of our hearts before God. When your heart is right, it doesn't matter as much what people think about you—even whether they think you're humble or not. If you are right with God, that is the thing. And there's freedom in that.

Humility typically looks a lot like great confidence. Because confidence, in truly humble people, comes not from themselves or through the promotion of their gifts. It comes from a dependence on Jesus and from a belief that this life is all about Him, and that everything we do, everything we say, and everything we are is about Him. It's not about us.

MEDITATE:
Do nothing from selfish ambition or conceit, but in humility count others more significant than yourselves. (Philippians 2:3)

REWIRE THE SPIRAL:
I choose to give God the credit for the gift of my life and all that is good in it.

God, I want the kind of confidence that comes from You and not from a false humility. Show me the peace that comes from choosing Your way over seeking importance for myself. Amen.

LIGHT SOURCE

THE WORLD'S MESSAGE IS SIMPLE: *YOU ARE ENOUGH. ALL ON YOUR OWN, you are enough.* But that mantra fails us—either because, deep down, we know we aren't enough or because our self-esteem inflates us to the point that we charge through life independent of God and people. Either outcome leaves us lonely and disappointed. Self-esteem is not the answer.

So why are we working so hard to do life, to make a difference, and to be great all on our own?

Scripture describes Jesus as the light shining into the darkness and becoming the light of men.[1] When I think about light, I realize that every single light humans have ever built requires energy or some force to light it. Flashlights, car lights, lamps—they all pull energy from some other source that can become drained or depleted.

Then I think of the light God creates. Fire, the sun, the stars all burning with great force—all the light He creates needs nothing to exist. It needs no other energy source. It just is.

1   See John 1:4–5.

When we find ourselves striving so hard to make a difference, to be enough, and to be important, it's as though we're trying to produce light on our own. And guess what happens when people try to produce anything in their own strength? We get tired. We experience a drain of energy, just like every man-made light that has ever been created.

So what if instead of trying to create light, we simply received light? That sounds so much more fun to me—and so much easier. We make lousy lights because we were built to enjoy and reflect light, not to produce it.

The vision of God for our lives is that we would receive His light and then give light to the world. In Matthew 5:14, Jesus says, "You are the light of the world." Most of the time the New Testament refers to Jesus as being the Light, but when His Spirit lives in us, *we* are the light of the world. We receive who Jesus is and then give that away.

The degree to which you believe and embrace your identity as a Spirit-filled child of God will be the degree to which His light shines through you. You are God's and He is yours. He is in you and through you and with you. That is your identity. And when you choose to embrace it, it changes everything.

If you embraced your true identity, you wouldn't just be able to rest from striving to do impossible things; you would be able to sit in awe of this fierce, crazy, awesome, and uncontainable Light that is fully accessible to you. With Jesus as your light source, you can stop spinning, and simply reflect the light He gives.

MEDITATE:
The light shines in the darkness, and the darkness has not overcome it. (John 1:5)

REWIRE THE SPIRAL:
I can rest from striving, and God can still move through me.

God, I want to know what it is to enjoy and reflect Your light, rather than trying so hard to create my own. Please shine on and through me today. Amen.

THE UPSIDE OF HUMILITY

WHEN WE REALIZE WE'VE BOUGHT INTO THE LIE OF OUR OWN GREAT-ness and make the shift to choose humility, we then can follow the example of Jesus, who was a walking, talking expression of humility before His Father God. When we do the same, we put God in His rightful place. We replace the lie of our greatness with the truth of who God is—and how needy we are apart from Him. Humility becomes the only logical posture of our hearts.

Yet sometimes humility doesn't feel good. For one, humility encourages us to let go of being awesome. And I want to be awesome! But the hard truth is, I'm not always awesome. I am going to make mistakes. I'm going to be selfish and sometimes unthoughtful and short. I'm going to let people down. Not that I'm excusing that behavior—I'm not going to *want* to do these things, but they will happen. How do I know? Because I'm just not all that great. Before you rush to my defense, **I think this understanding is the goal: caring little about what others think about me, or even what I think about me.** Because the need to be awesome is not something positive; it's an impossible weight and pressure we put on ourselves—one we can never measure up to. Humility allows us to cast off that weight of striving for awesomeness and just be who we were created to be. Doesn't that sound freeing?

I know that it's all the rage these days to talk about how amazing everyone is, how we're each *special* and *talented* and *enough.* But I have to tell you, I don't find these ideas in Scripture. We find our "enoughness" only in Christ. If anything, God's Word tells us that when we're weak, it's actually a good thing, because Christ's power is made more evident in our weakness.

I happen to think that this is *fantastic* news.

Listen, there's a reason we wear ourselves out posturing. There's a reason we buy stuff labeled "antiaging." There's a reason we drive more car than we can afford. There's a reason we notice labels.

We all want to be awesome, even though Christ is the only awesome one.

This is one of the most freeing and rarely embraced truths of following Christ: Because of the sacrifice of Jesus, we get His awesomeness as part of the deal. We get forgiveness. We get rest. We get grace for our souls.

Humility reminds us of this truth. It says, "Relax. Your only hope is Jesus." This good news grants us the exhale we all are craving.

MEDITATE:
When I am weak, then I am strong. (2 Corinthians 12:10)

REWIRE THE SPIRAL:
I don't need to be awesome, because Jesus is.

God, it's a relief to not have to be awesome before You. Your awesomeness is enough for me. Please help me choose to let go, receive, and relax in You today. Amen.

NOTHING TO PROVE

EVERY ONCE IN A WHILE, I FIND MYSELF AROUND SOMEONE WHOSE soul is full of God. Whose soul is so content, Jesus is just pouring out of them. Do you know people like that? It is so refreshing. So beautiful. People like that are not needy. They're not trying to prove themselves. They're not trying to measure up. They're not trying to get your attention or affection. They hold no judgment for others because they are aware of their own sin. They've chosen humility, and it has set them free.

My grandmother lived this way. She was at home in her skin and put others at ease as well. She was self-deprecating and deeply aware of her own shortcomings. As her grandkids, we did so many things over the years that should have disappointed her. She should have judged us and told us how out of line we were. But she always left the judging to God and pulled us in all the closer.

She knew grace and she gave it away. It all was rooted in her under-standing of the amazing grace that saved a wretch like her. Faith and the gospel were simple and real to her. She didn't need to wax eloquent over theological points; she just chose to love, to never speak ill, to believe the best, and to let God be God. No need to try to be a god when He was plenty good at His job.

Something about her core identity was altogether different than most of the world's. She wasn't trying to impress anyone. She also wasn't defined by or in bondage to her sin. She was forgiven and free, and her life gave that away. The kind of humility that brings life and peace. Fed on God's grace.

Grace breathes more grace.

What kind of person are you?

Are you impressive? Or are you broken? Or forgiven?

The Gospels tell us the story of Jesus washing His disciples' feet. When God, who owns every universe, made Himself less. When the teacher became a servant. His identity drove His humility. Jesus was the Son of the Almighty God; He was clear and secure in that fact. Therefore, there was nothing He was grasping for. He had nothing to prove in that society or to these men.

When you have nothing to protect and nothing to prove, God moves through you. When you have nothing to protect and nothing to prove, you know freedom. That's the power of humility.

MEDITATE:
Then [Jesus] poured water into a basin and began to wash the disciples' feet and to wipe them with the towel that was wrapped around him. (John 13:5)

REWIRE THE SPIRAL:
I have nothing to prove.

God, my soul longs for the simple contentment and freedom that comes from letting go of my self-interest. Help me choose humility as a way of life, surrounded by Your grace. Amen.

AN UNLIKELY PLEASURE

HERE'S THE THING. I BELIEVE THE BIBLE. I WANT TO LIVE WHAT IT SAYS. When it tells me to live like Jesus and to humble myself, I want to do so. I really do. But despite these noble intentions, the fact is, I can't conjure humility myself. The practice of humility is inextricably connected to the practice of being still and seeking God. We can't become more like Him apart from Him imparting Himself to us. Humility comes only when I choose to be with Him and depend on Him instead of buying the lie that I am enough.

A favorite Bible dictionary of mine defines humility this way: "A condition of lowliness or affliction in which one experiences a loss of power and prestige." It then clarifies the definition with this: "Outside of biblical faith, humility in this sense would not usually be considered a virtue. Within the context of the Judeo-Christian tradition, however, humility is considered the proper attitude of human beings toward their Creator. Humility is a grateful and spontaneous awareness that life is a gift, and it is manifested as an ungrudging and unhypocritical acknowledgment of absolute dependence upon God."[1]

Outside of biblical faith, humility would be *lunacy*. Who wants *less* power, *less* prestige? But within biblical faith, this utter dependence on God is the goal.

If God created me and loves me, why would I want to steal any of His glory? I can't steal His glory, because who ever could—but why would I even try?

The truth is, our hearts aren't really after power; they're after joy. And the deception we buy into is that somehow joy will come when we have power. But joy comes when we lay aside our power and rest in God's.

My prayer for myself—and also for you—is that we'd be utterly dependent on God, more and more, even as we stumble and get back up again. That we'd seek Him and find Him and learn from Him and lean into Him, that we'd be in this world as Jesus Himself was. That we'd accept every invitation into humility, prizing the needs of others above our own. That we wouldn't despise that which will mature us by reminding us to bow lower, and lower still. In fact, that we'd welcome and even take pleasure in what humbles us, because we know the freedom it brings. Though a lofty goal, this utter dependence on God is such a freed-up way of thinking about our circumstances and the people around us, and it is such a beautiful choice.

---

1   *Tyndale Bible Dictionary*, s.v. "humility," ed. Walter A. Elwell and Philip W. Comfort (Wheaton, IL: Tyndale, 2001), 618.

MEDITATE:

Humble yourselves, therefore, under the mighty hand of God so that at the proper time he may exalt you. (1 Peter 5:6)

REWIRE THE SPIRAL:

I choose God's sufficiency over my own power.

Father, I choose to seek You and be with You. Teach my heart to bow low in response to Your glory. Amen.

GOOD STUFF INSIDE

I LOVE GETTING AMAZON PACKAGES. THERE'S ALWAYS A LITTLE CHRIST-mas thrill when I open the bag, even if it's lightbulbs or something mundane like that.

I was listening to my friend Earle preach, and he pointed out that as followers of Christ, we're the Amazon bag. The kind with the pull tab. We carry the good thing, but we are the bag—we're not the main event. Nobody is going to the door and thinking to themselves, *Oh my gosh, look at this bag that just arrived at my house! What a gorgeous paper bag.* They're going for the contents. And the contents of our lives should be the mind of Christ. That means the mind of someone who is willing to lay down their life, willing to be emptied out, willing to be humbled to the point of embarrassment or misunderstanding or even, in Christ's case, death. The contents of our lives should be the fruit of Christ because we have the mind of Christ. That's what should be known of us.

Why should we be motivated to live this way? It sounds miserable on the outside. Yet it's really the freest way to live. When we don't care so much about our own importance, we're free to enjoy and cheer for others. That's the posture you get to experience with humility. You can know, *I'm not in this to impress. I'm not in this to perform. I'm in this for the glory of God. I'm in this to love.*

The other thing that comes with humility is that God's greatness is revealed. As Scripture says, at the name of Jesus, every knee will bow. So the ultimate goal of humility is that people would see God—God in us—and they'd see God's glory because of our obedience. All the striving and posturing in the world is not going to steal an ounce of the glory of God. But what can steal the glory of God in our lives is pride. And that's a state of the heart. That's not a state of your actions, of your words, or of people's opinions about you. That is a state of your mind and your thoughts. Honestly, only you and God can work that out together.

Ask yourself, *In this situation, do I care more about what people think about me than I care what they think about God?* Ask regularly and, just as often, remember to choose the better way. Choose to be the package that brings the good stuff to people—the contents of the mind of Christ.

MEDITATE:
That at the name of Jesus every knee should bow, in heaven and on earth and under the earth, and every tongue confess that Jesus Christ is Lord, to the glory of God the Father.
(Philippians 2:10–11)

REWIRE THE SPIRAL:
I can take the pressure off myself when I choose pleasing God over pleasing people.

God, thank You for offering a better way than always needing to impress. Please let Your goodness be visible through me today. Amen.

LAYING DOWN OUR LIVES

OUR HEARTS AREN'T ACTUALLY AFTER POWER OR IMPORTANCE. OUR hearts are after joy. We're built for it. That's what we want. The deception that we buy into, somehow, is that joy will come if we get known, if we get power, or if we become important. But what Scripture says is that joy comes when we lay down our lives. It's the opposite. Joy only comes when we lay down everything on earth that we think matters. When we lay down our name, when we lay down being understood, when we lay down even our own lives, joy and freedom come through. And that is a supernatural reality. One you won't fully understand until you've tasted it.

When you've tasted it, though, a funny thing happens. A feeling of loss washes over you like a wave: *Oh, I just gave up something on earth.* But when the wave pulls back out, something new is there: *I'm okay. Yes, somebody misunderstands me. I'm not important to them. That's hurtful. But I'm okay because I'm loved and I'm known by God, and my hope is secure.* That is the joy of self-forgetfulness. Freedom comes when we are not the center of our own minds or our own lives.

The most direct way to get to this place of self-forgetfulness is to go out and serve others. Love other people in action. Put other people's needs before our own. We can't sit here and *will* selflessness into being. It comes as we serve people, as we actually get up out of our chairs and clear the table. As we love and welcome our neighbors. As we go to the local elderly home and visit and get to know people. As we think about other people more than ourselves. When we do that, we become more obsessed with what God is doing in other people's lives than what He's not doing in ours. We realize that loving other people is so much better than loving ourselves—so much freedom and joy comes because of it.

So today I want you to do something crazy. Love somebody that you would not normally love. Decide together with your friends to go love people. Take a family food, go out to coffee together, have someone over, mow a neighbor's lawn—just go love people in a radical way. It's incredibly fun, because there are a million different ways to love your neighbors. So do something for someone today, and watch your mind shift from being absorbed with yourself to loving other people. I'm telling you, that's where the freedom is.

MEDITATE:

By this we know love, that he laid down his life for us, and we ought to lay down our lives for the brothers. (1 John 3:16)

REWIRE THE SPIRAL:

I can experience the joy of self-forgetfulness when I serve others.

Jesus, thank You for the people You've put in my path. Please lead me to someone You would have me help today and let me sense Your love for them. Thank You for making me part of a plan so much bigger than me. Amen.

DAY

56

REMEMBER WHO YOU ARE

OUR MINDS SPIN AND SPIN, OFTEN GRABBING HOLD OF LIES IN THE search for stability. Messages get mixed, and it feels as though we can't quite put our feet back down on the simple truth of what it means to love Jesus, and what it means to be loved by Jesus.

If you need to be reminded of who Jesus says you are, may I take your hand and tell you again what He says about who He is, and therefore who you are?

"I AM WHO I AM."[1] "I am . . . the beginning and the end." "I am . . . the first and the last."[2] I am light; in Me there is no darkness at all.[3] "My hand laid the foundation of the earth, and my right hand spread out the heavens; when I call to them, they stand forth together."[4] "Before I formed you in the womb I knew you."[5] "I chose you and appointed you that you should go and bear fruit and that your fruit should abide, so that whatever you ask the Father in my name, he may give it to you."[6] I am He who blots out your mistakes, and I will not remember your sins.[7] To

---

1   Exodus 3:14.   3   See 1 John 1:5.   5   Jeremiah 1:5.   7   See Isaiah 43:25.
2   Revelation 22:13.   4   Isaiah 48:13.   6   John 15:16.

all who receive Me, who believe in My name, I give the right to become children of God.[8] "Do you not know that you are God's temple and that God's Spirit dwells in you?"[9] My Spirit is within you.[10] I will not leave you.[11] I will equip you for every good work I've planned.[12] I did not give you a spirit of fear but of power, love, and self-control.[13] I will build My church through you, and the gates of hell will not overcome it.[14] I will comfort you as you wait.[15] I will remind you this is all real.[16] I am on My way.[17] My steadfast love endures forever and ever.[18] In just a little while, I am coming.[19] I will take you to the place I am.[20] You will inherit the earth.[21] You will be with Me. I will wipe every tear from your eyes, and death will be no more. "Behold, I am making all things new."[22] My kingdom is coming. My will will be done on earth as it is in heaven.[23]

All these things are true for you and for anyone who loves and follows Jesus. This is who we are because of whose we are. And our God doesn't change, and He always delivers on His promises.

MEDITATE:
To all who did receive him, who believed in his name, he gave the right to become children of God. (John 1:12)

REWIRE THE SPIRAL:
My identity is secure in God.

God, as I go into this day, remind me who You are and who I am because of You. Let my mind rest on that. Amen.

8   See John 1:12.
9   1 Corinthians 3:16.
10 See Ezekiel 36:27.
11 See Deuteronomy 31:8.
12 See Hebrews 13:21.
13 See 2 Timothy 1:7.
14 See Matthew 16:18.
15 See Isaiah 66:13.
16 See John 14:26.
17 See Revelation 3:11.
18 See Psalm 138:8.
19 See Hebrews 10:37.
20 See John 14:3.
21 See Psalm 25:13.
22 See Revelation 21:3–5.
23 See Matthew 6:10.

EMOTION

Self-pity

THOUGHT

I am a victim to my circumstances

BEHAVIOR

Complains

RELATIONSHIPS

Places blame

CONSEQUENCE

Consistently unhappy

CONSEQUENCE

Joyful

RELATIONSHIPS

Forgiving

BEHAVIOR

Gives thanks

THOUGHT

My circumstances are an opportunity to experience God

I choose to be grateful no matter what life brings ⟶

EMOTION

Self-pity

FROM
VICTIMHOOD
TO
GRATEFULNESS

THE CONTRAST

IF THERE'S ONE THING THAT STRIKES ME ABOUT THE APOSTLE PAUL, IT'S that he was thankful—so thankful. Despite all the crazy stuff he went through, he was thankful for his fellow believers, thankful for the diligence of his co-workers, and thankful for where he was stationed even though it was a cold, dark prison cell. The man was minding his mind.

I can't help but be struck by the contrast between Paul's and my mind some days.

Paul had been imprisoned for preaching the gospel, yet despite this unjust treatment, he saw fit to give thanks. He saw fit to keep praying, to keep ministering, to keep striving alongside fellow believers for the hearts of women and men.

What do we so often see fit to do? If we're honest: *complain.*

But we can shift our thinking. We can see life in a new way. If it's our work we're complaining about, for example, we can change how we view work. We can see our co-workers with fresh eyes, forge real relationships with them, and watch for ways to care for and serve them. We can interact differently with the people we encounter, seeing them not as strangers but as real people with real stories who might need real grace. We can use our commute time to pray.

A friend of mine resented her job, but after she tried these new practices for a month, she told me that she no longer despised it. In fact, she *loved* it. Instead of fixating on the unfairness of her circumstance and stewing over how she deserved something better, she began to see her less-than-fulfilling job as an opportunity to advance the kingdom. God had set her in a strategic place to love others, and now she was excited to be part of His plan. Instead of looking for things to complain about, my friend was looking for reasons to give thanks. She didn't know it at the time, but she was doing herself far greater favors than merely ensuring a more pleasant workday. She was *rewiring her brain* by choosing gratitude. She was allowing God to remake her, body and mind.

That's what gratitude does for us. It snaps us out of the lie, *I am a victim to my circumstances.* The truth is, *My circumstances provide opportunities to experience the goodness of God.* You can choose to be grateful, and like Paul and my friend did, you can shift the spiral of victimhood into something wonderful.

I thank my God in all my remembrance of you, always in every prayer of mine for you all making my prayer with joy, because of your partnership in the gospel from the first day until now. **(Philippians 1:3–5)**

When I choose gratefulness, I stop the negative spiral of victimhood.

God, I want to try a new way of thinking. Please remake me and help me rise beyond my circumstances today. Amen.

YOUR BRAIN ON GRATITUDE

VICTIMHOOD IS ONE OF THE MOST PARALYZING ENEMIES OF OUR MINDS. It keeps us fixated on something other than the God of the universe, and convinces us of the lie that we are at the mercy of our circumstances.

But we have a choice. We can center our thoughts on the certainty that, no matter what comes, we are upheld securely by God's righteous right hand.

And that will shift our minds toward gratitude.

Research shows us that gratefulness has a reviving effect on the part of your brain that controls bodily functions—eating, drinking, sleeping, the whole works.[1] So doing something as straightforward as saying "Thank you" is like a tune-up for your inner world.

Additionally, expressing gratitude causes an increase in dopamine hits, the reward neurotransmitter that makes the brain happy. In studies, each time a subject expressed gratitude, the brain basically said, "Ooh!

---

1   Alex Korb, "The Grateful Brain: The Neuroscience of Giving Thanks," *Psychology Today*, November 20, 2012, www.psychologytoday.com/us/blog/prefrontal-nudity/201211/the-grateful-brain.

Do it again!" Feeling gratitude led to feeling more gratitude, which led to feeling more and more gratitude still.[2] It's a positive spiral.

So what happens when you make gratitude a practice?

1. **Your relationships get healthier.** Something as simple as saying "Thanks" to an acquaintance makes that person more likely to seek friendship with you.

2. **Your body gets healthier.** Grateful people exercise more, make better decisions about their health, and report having fewer aches and pains.

3. **Your mind gets healthier.** Gratitude reduces toxic emotions such as envy, frustration, and regret.

4. **You get nicer.** One study found that "grateful people are more likely to behave in a prosocial manner," which I think is a nice way of saying, "A grateful person is less likely to be a jerk."

5. **Your sleep gets healthier**, which is a good enough reason for you and me to be grateful.

6. **You become more confident.** Gratitude allows a person to genuinely celebrate the achievements of others instead of wishing she'd been the one to succeed.

7. **Your mental strength improves**, helping you reduce stress, overcome trauma, and increase resilience even during bad times.

---

2   Korb, "Grateful Brain."

Gratitude is good for us—God designed us that way. With everything it gives us, no wonder it's part of His prescription for a freer mind.

CHOOSE THANKS

EVER WONDER WHY SOME PEOPLE SEEM HAPPIER THAN YOU, EVEN IF they are going through more difficult circumstances? Maybe you have visited Christians in developing countries, thinking you were there to minister to them in their need, only to realize through their joy and self-lessness that *you* were the one who had the need. Yeah, me too.

When Paul wrote his letter to the Philippians, the greatest exposi-tion on joy ever written, he was actually bound in chains under house arrest. Paul understood something that we in our cocoon of comfort in the West rarely realize. He understood that because we have been made new creations, we have the Spirit's power and the freedom to choose. Changing our minds *is* possible. We do not have to spin out in nega-tive spirals—because we know our happiness is anchored in something greater than anything we can see here and now.

So this prompts a second question: What are you looking to for hap-piness? Whether it is opioids or people's praise, whatever causes you to experience strong emotions of either happiness or disappointment—that is likely the thing you are living for. And it is very likely ruining your life.

If all Paul saw were his circumstances and his inability to end his imprisonment, he would surely have been despondent. But his circumstances didn't dictate his thoughts. It was his love of Jesus and his trust in a good, loving, in-control God that consumed his mind and gave him purpose. And the same Spirit that empowered Paul to trust in the direst circumstances—the same power, incidentally, that raised Christ from the dead—is fully accessible to you and me. Right now.

As we make the shift from debilitating lines of thinking to thoughts that are helpful and God-honoring and wise, we can make the choice to be *grateful.* God made sure to include a clear call to thankfulness in Scripture because He knows that only when we're planted in the soil of gratitude will we learn and grow and thrive. So we can be people who consistently and sincerely give thanks, regardless of our wounded pasts or the circumstances we presently face. We can say, "I choose to be grateful."

MEDITATE:
Rejoice always, pray without ceasing, give thanks in all circumstances; for this is the will of God in Christ Jesus for you.
(1 Thessalonians 5:16–18)

REWIRE THE SPIRAL:
Because of Jesus, I can choose to see the good around me in spite of my circumstances.

God, thank You that, no matter what is going on in my life today, I can make a choice to be renewed and to embrace gratefulness. Let thanks flow out of me, regardless of my circumstances. Amen.

SURVIVORS

SOME OF MY FAVORITE PEOPLE ARE THE ONES WHO HAVE SUFFERED THE most. My friend Julie seems to have more joy than almost anyone else I know, and yet she also has suffered with health struggles and difficult circumstances more than almost anyone else I know.

Here's the truth: We can observe our suffering without being overtaken by our suffering. We can *see* it without becoming its slave.

That doesn't mean we shouldn't fight against suffering in the world. Scripture *commands* us to fight, in fact.[1] But in Christ, we can fight not from a place of insecurity and outrage but from a place of reconciliation. Of calm confidence. Of peace. Why? Because our victory is sure. We've already won.

We live in a day when true injustices are being named, brought into the light, and, on occasion, overcome and made right. I love this. God loves this. Fighting racism, speaking out against sexual and physical abuse inside and outside the church, advocating for the welfare of the

---

1   Micah 6:8; Luke 18:7; Proverbs 31:9.

vulnerable—these causes are of utmost importance to Jesus. They must also be to us.

There are very real oppressors out there. Yet there is a lot we can do. We can help those who have been "victimized" once and for all break free. More and more often we hear the term *survivors* instead of *victims,* and it's an important shift. To define ourselves by others' wrongdoing is to render ourselves helpless and weak. To turn over our power to them only binds us up.

Yes, it's tempting to define ourselves by what we've endured. But if I'm learning one thing, it's that there is an altogether better way.

My friend Sarah has suffered racist attacks all her life, even in a church. But she blew my mind when she said, "I am choosing to trust again." She went on to launch a series of racial reconciliation conversations in our church that are bringing people together for real change. I look at her impact, and I think, *How could someone so abused and wronged turn back to the very people who hurt her and say, "I want to build a bridge to get back to you. I want to try again"?*

Sarah would say: *Jesus.*

Jesus shifts everything. In Jesus, we can acknowledge our frustration, pain, and suffering without abdicating our peace and joy. **In Jesus, we can change where we fight *from* without changing what we fight *for.*** By His power, we can show that, regardless of how grim the situation, God is in the business of redeeming *all* things. And from that place of grateful confidence, we can reach out, we can trust, and we can love.

MEDITATE:

He has told you, O man, what is good; and what does the LORD require of you but to do justice, and to love kindness, and to walk humbly with your God? (Micah 6:8)

REWIRE THE SPIRAL:

My struggles in life do not define me.

Jesus, thank You that the worst things that have happened to me don't define me. Teach me about Your justice and lead me in Your way. I am so grateful that You make redemption possible. Amen.

GIFTS WE DIDN'T ASK FOR

SO MANY TIMES, WHEN I'VE SEEN THE SUFFERING OF THOSE I LOVE, I remember that I don't always like God's plans. When loved ones have wrestled with broken marriages and broken promises, with diagnoses and despair, with layoffs at work and lethargy in motherhood, with aging parents and angsty preteens, God's plans haven't felt especially benevolent. In those moments, life feels cruel at best.

And yet.

Haven't we known God more intimately *because of* our difficulties? Don't we carve out new capacity for believing God when we're on our knees on those dark days? Don't we learn to let people help us, because without help we just can't succeed? Haven't our blessings felt sweeter than they would have if we had not felt their lack? Don't you and I look back on the roughest of times and see that they have brought the most profound growth?

This may seem like an impossibly sunny outlook to adopt, especially amid suffering. It may strike you as cold comfort during the worst of it. I know the sinking feeling that comes when someone blithely tries to force a silver lining on you in a situation that has shattered your heart. I'm not here to do that. But there is a light at the end of the tunnel, and a strength that comes from endurance. Endurance and character and Spirit-enabled hope—these are marks of ones who choose gratitude even, and especially, in the hard times.

It's like creating a piece of pottery that's fired in a kiln to make it strong and watertight. You work so hard on that clay and then put the piece into the fire, having no idea how it will turn out. Later, you open the kiln and hold your breath, wondering if it will have broken into a million pieces or turned into the most beautiful thing you've seen. Those really are the only two options, aren't they? Not only for pottery but also for us. When we walk through the fires we inevitably find in life, will we emerge fortified or falling apart?

It's all part of the choice we make. I'd bet, if you looked back on your worst times, it wouldn't take you long to pinpoint the strengths you've gained through them—even if you legitimately wish those things had never happened. There's no way we're going to ever be grateful *for* the bad times. But when they happen, we can choose gratefulness *through* them, despite them, in faith that God has not abandoned us. This is not about a blindly positive attitude or forcing a bad situation to be good. It's about leaning on the strength and love of a God who is more powerful than it all, and who has our good at heart.

MEDITATE:
We rejoice in our sufferings, knowing that suffering produces endurance, and endurance produces character, and character produces hope, and hope does not put us to shame, because God's love has been poured into our hearts through the Holy Spirit who has been given to us. (Romans 5:3–5)

REWIRE THE SPIRAL:
I can choose to look for unexpected gifts even when I'm not where I want to be.

Heavenly Father, help me choose wisely. May I be found praising You, even while standing in the flames. Amen.

PURPOSE BEHIND THE PAIN

THE SHIFT FROM VICTIMHOOD TO GRATITUDE TAKES BRAVERY. BUT WHEN we do it, we affirm our understanding that *God remains committed to redeeming all things.*

Paul told the Philippians he was sure that everything that had happened to him had happened for a specific purpose. That purpose, you might guess, was to spread the gospel—God's good news of love and grace.

By choosing gratitude over victimhood, Paul was able to center his thoughts on God's purpose behind the pain. He could focus on the impact of his imprisonment, which involved the palace guard coming to know Christ. He could see that his ministry was far from over; in fact, it was only beginning.

But to see God's good purposes, we have to focus our gaze beyond our immediate situations. We have to remember that, even now, we have a choice. We can choose to praise and honor God right where we are. We can trust that we serve a God who is both *transcendent* and *immanent*—fancy words for saying that His ways are beyond human understanding[1] and also that God chooses to be near us, to be with us, even in the hardest times when we cannot yet see how He could possibly bring anything good from our circumstances.

But what if God's plans include a grueling divorce, massive health problems, children leaving us, our families being uprooted, or a season of darkness that doesn't seem to shift? In the moment, when news of the stroke comes, when the decision is made to relocate, when doubt threatens to take us out—do we think God's plans are good then too?

I'm reminded of an experience a friend of mine went through when she lost her husband to a cruel battle with ALS. I asked whether she'd been mad at God at any point, given the tragedy she'd endured. The concept was so foreign to her that she seemed offended I'd even asked. "Mad at God?" she said. "You know, we never once asked, 'Why?' If anything, we asked 'Why *not*?'" She said their faith in Jesus assured them that God would use even his disease and eventual death for good. Her husband did proclaim Jesus to the very end, even from his wheelchair through a voice simulator. God has used it. And God still is using it.

"I still don't fully accept that he is gone, never to come back," she said. "But this much I do know: His death was not an ending but an extension. And I'm determined to stick around to find out what that extension involves."

My friend knows that God's not done with her or her husband's story. And He's not done with yours either. Whatever you've gone through and whatever you've faced, He is in the business of redeeming it all.

---

1 Isaiah 55:9.

MEDITATE:

I want you to know, brothers, that what has happened to me has really served to advance the gospel, so that it has become known throughout the whole imperial guard and to all the rest that my imprisonment is for Christ. (Philippians 1:12–13)

REWIRE THE SPIRAL:

God will redeem everything that happens to me.

God, Your plans are unknowable, but I trust that they are good. You are a redeemer through and through. I choose to center my thoughts on You and see what You will do. Amen.

CONQUERORS

WHAT WOULD HAPPEN IF WE STARTED TRULY BELIEVING WE HAVE RE-sponsibility, authority, and power over our lives? Imagine how energizing that would be! On the flip side, we become paralyzed when we start to believe we are victims to our lives, our circumstances, our thoughts, our feelings, and our situations. We become defeated. We become sad, sad, sad.

All of us have taken up this banner of victimhood in some way. It might be due to a small thing. It might be because of a relationship in which we've been wounded. It might be because of a circumstance that just feels so unfair. Whatever it is, we own this idea that we have been so wronged—maybe even to the point of being *proud* of it. But that is a miserable way to live.

God has given us so much authority and power over our circum-stances, over our feelings, over our minds, and over our attitudes. He has given us the freedom to choose and to change. So we don't have to live as victims.

I want to be super clear. I'm not saying there are not real victims. Some of you have been victimized to an unthinkable level. If you have been abused, wounded, or hurt by people, I am so, so sorry. Nobody's going to diminish or dismiss that or treat it flippantly. My heart aches for you and with you, just as my heart aches for those whose stories absolutely punch me in the gut.

What I'm speaking to here is the victimhood mentality many of us have that sucks us into a spiral of thinking we have been wronged, that life isn't fair, and that it's us against the world. I'm talking about the victimhood that comes when we don't realize the part we've played in a situation we're annoyed with. I'm talking about the victimhood that steals the power of God from a situation. I'm talking about the victimhood that claims we're helpless and hopeless, when God has said, "I've made you more than conquerors."

As we know from the Bible, God has equipped us with the divine gifts of courage and sound minds so we can stand against the powers of evil and injustice in the world, so we are not victims to our lives. We're not victims to our minds. We're not victims to a "poor me" mentality that emerges from our stubborn will.

Even if you struggle with victimhood from real, serious illness and hurt and abuse and crimes, you can still choose something other than a defeatist attitude so you don't lose all your joy. You can still believe God for healing, a future, and a hope. Gratitude is a weapon you can use to fight against any situation the enemy throws at you, and you can choose it. You have that power right now, and no one can take it away from you.

In all these things we are more than conquerors through him who loved us. **(Romans 8:37)**

With God's power, I am not a victim.

God, please fill me with the conviction of the power You've given me to assert authority over my own life, my own thoughts, my own heart. I choose to use what You've given me. Amen.

EVEN IF

IN PSALM 119, WE SEE KING DAVID FACING VICIOUS SLANDER AND threats against his life. Astonishingly, though, his answer was, *You know what? God is my defender. I'm not going to be the one to defend my own name. God will defend me.* And in the end, God did defend him. But in the midst of it, David wasn't immediately rescued. One of the people tearing him down was his own son, fighting against him and trying to take over the throne. I cannot imagine how much that hurt. But we see in the psalms that David continued to trust God and say, *Even if all this falls apart, God, You are good—even if.*

In so many circumstances, we are presented with the choice to say to God, "Even if the worst thing happens to me, You are good. So I'm not going to live in weakness and in distress. I'm going to live in power with authority." But do we take that opportunity?

It's one thing to claim our authority in life, and it's another to treat it as a magic spell. Now, the word *authority* can get used wrongly. It's one thing to flippantly say we can just speak with authority over our cancer or over our circumstance, and that it'll go away. God can do that, of course—I've seen Him do it. He can heal. But we can also have authority in the reality of knowing that our ultimate hope and healing is in heaven, and that wrongs will be made right—even if they're not made right until heaven. So even though we can't always control how everything works out here, we can speak with authority because our eternity is set.

What does it look like to trust God with authority and with power? To believe the truth about ourselves and our future? That's going to take war. You've got to fight back against the spirals of victimhood. You can't just passively get over it and try to think positively. When you are going through something where you feel beaten up or backed into a corner, where you feel helpless or hopeless, I want you to start noticing—noticing the good in people, noticing the good from God, and noticing the good in your life. And maybe you'll get to a place where you can say, "Oh, you know what? Everything is not going to hell in a handbasket. I actually see God advocating for me. I see good happening around me. I see good in myself. I see myself being stronger than I was yesterday. I see myself getting up today and taking care of my kids when I didn't think I could breathe."

Eventually you'll realize how strong you are, how strong God has made you, how good He has been to you, and how much He's watching out for you. It is a supernaturally different way to live.

MEDITATE:
Though the cords of the wicked ensnare me, I do not forget your law. . . . You are good and do good. (Psalm 119:61, 68)

REWIRE THE SPIRAL:
God is good, even if the worst happens.

God, You are my defender, and You are good. Thank You for hope, power, and the ability to overcome. Help me choose to notice Your goodness today. Amen.

DAY

65

THE LOOK OF GRACE

OF ALL THE BATTLES WE FIGHT FOR OUR MIND, VICTIMHOOD MIGHT BE the most visible spiral. After all, people can see when we're feeling beset and defeated. I can tell in the posture of my son, when walking out from school, if he is walking out as someone who got picked on all day or as someone who has chosen joy. Every day is about the same for a fifth-grade boy—kids smack-talk every day. The difference is not in what was said to him that day. It's in how he handled it.

The same thing goes for us. We may not see if we're exuding defeat, but we can ask bold questions of our friends: *Do you see me being a victim to my circumstances, to my mind, or to my emotions?* Ask that question to people who know you really well and be ready for the answer. And then own it. You've got to say, *Okay, what does it look like for me not to live as a victim to this?*

For one of my kids, this is a major struggle. And the answer involves bringing them back to grace and reminding them what it means to be forgiven. I say, "My child, yes, there are plenty of times when you have been wronged in life, but gosh, think of how many times we have wronged God and how much He has come for us." He comes for us every time, no matter what, with His infinite resources of grace. And ultimately, that's what we all stand on.

That's where grace takes root—in those who have been forgiven much. The more we're in touch with our gratitude, and the more we remember how much we've been forgiven by our infinitely loving God, the more we will be able to forgive other people.

In practice, this results in free, joyful, peaceful people who aren't out of touch with what's been done to them but are in touch with what God has done for them. And here's where it gets miraculous: when you move in reconciliation toward the very people who hurt you. That movement can only come from an explosion of the Spirit, because people just don't have a category for this kind of reconciliation. It screams of a God that issues hope beyond our understanding. That miraculous kind of spirit is just as visible as a spirit of defeat. It comes from choosing to receive healing from God instead of staying in victimhood. And it looks like a peace that can only come from God Himself.

MEDITATE:
Let us then with confidence draw near to the throne of grace, that we may receive mercy and find grace to help in time of need. (Hebrews 4:16)

God, thank You that I can stand on Your grace and keep coming back for more mercy. I choose to let that pour out of me, instead of defeat. By Your Spirit, issue Your hope to my heart. Amen.

REWIRE THE SPIRAL:
I will choose mercy instead of defeat.

DAY
66

THE GOOD FIGHT

MY HUSBAND'S GRANDFATHER, WHO'S IN HIS NINETIES, FOUGHT IN World War II. His parachute didn't open when he was dropped out of an airplane. He crashed and blacked out, and ended up in a prisoner-of-war camp in Germany. It was dark and it was horrible. He lost fingers and nearly his life. He had everything stacked against him. And yet, having survived, he said, "No. I'm going to go be a great husband. I'm going to build a great life. I'm going to obey God. I'm going to raise my kids to love God. I'm going to be a good man."

I watch his life and I think, *Okay, that is what it looks like to slay the darkness.* It's slaying the things that would cripple us and make us bitter and completely cranky. That's fighting the good fight—it's choosing delight and joy and gratitude instead of cynicism and victimhood.

We slay the darkness by choosing joy over choosing to spiral downward because life isn't fair. And I'm not saying life hasn't been really unfair to you. Goodness gracious. In my time in ministry I've heard so many prayer requests for things I can't even stomach or imagine. So I'm not dismissing this pain. I'm saying there is a God that's bigger than it, and that living as a victim to it is not an option.

This is something so many others, like my husband's grandfather, preach so much better than me because they have tasted darkness and brokenness beyond anything I could ever imagine. But I have watched him up close, and I can tell you, he has chosen gratitude. And God has protected his joy, his delight, and his heart. He hasn't grown bitter or angry. He's found that forgiveness is a better way to live.

So you have a choice. Consider your thoughts with the certainty that no matter what comes, you are upheld securely by God's righteous right hand. Refusing to be a slave to your circumstances doesn't mean that you gloss over them. You acknowledge the frustration, the pain, and the injustice. You look it squarely in the face, but you do that without losing your joy or your peace. Because you know that, ultimately, Jesus has the power to right all wrongs. And He has won the fight.

MEDITATE:
Fear not, for I am with you; be not dismayed, for I am your God; I will strengthen you, I will help you, I will uphold you with my righteous right hand. (Isaiah 41:10)

REWIRE THE SPIRAL:
Gratitude slays the darkness around me.

Father, I want to slay the darkness in my heart and mind. Please give me the resolve to fight in Your strength, upheld by Your hand. Amen.

THE SMALL, SIMPLE THINGS

YOU AND I ARE ENGAGED IN A REAL BATTLE. THE BATTLE FOR OUR MINDS and for souls on this earth is no joke. It can feel overwhelming. Yet compared to the fierceness of the fight, the way we move forward is awfully simple and not what you might expect. You ready?

We do the simple things Jesus said to do.

What did He say to do?

Pray.

Hold tightly to His Word.

Love Him with all of our heart, soul, mind, and strength instead of pretending we do.

Love our neighbor.

So simple. He didn't say fight every cultural battle of our day, because He knew the fights of this world will pass away. No matter how important the cultural fight is, guess what? In heaven it will not matter. Instead, we fight for truth, and for people to believe God. In fact, it all boils down to this: abide and love.

Jesus essentially says, *Listen. Stick with Me, abide with Me, pray, read the Word, be with Me, love Me, and stay near. I'll work in you.* He has a big vision for us, but He will cause the big part to happen.

So what do we do? The simple stuff.

So simple that you can actually know what to do when you feel yourself struggling and spiraling. When you feel yourself moving into that place of *What do I do? I feel paralyzed and don't know what to do.* Choose to meet with Him. To hold on to Him.

Do you know what happens when you go to meet with Jesus? When you are with Him in His presence? When you are in His Word and memorizing it? When you are in your local church and in authentic community, and you're honest about the struggles in your mind instead of avoiding them?

No darkness can stand against you.

Nothing can stand against the force of God moving through a soul completely in love with Him.

It is the simple things that will change the world.

It is the old, unclever things that will change your soul.

So sit down every day with Him in His Word, look eye to eye with a small group of people, and tell the truth about your soul. Do the simple work of loving God and loving people. It is messy, hard, and not too glamorous. But that sounds like Jesus.

Love the Lord your God with all your heart and with all your soul and with all your mind and with all your strength. . . . "You shall love your neighbor as yourself." (Mark 12:30–31)

My small decisions matter.

God, I need Your simplicity in my life. When I feel overwhelmed or helpless, draw me back to the small, simple things, and to Your presence. Amen.

EMOTION
Shame

CONSEQUENCE
Known

THOUGHT
I can solve problems on my own

RELATIONSHIPS
Connected

BEHAVIOR
Builds walls

BEHAVIOR
Builds bridges

RELATIONSHIPS
Isolated

THOUGHT
God made me to live known and loved

I choose to be known ⟶

CONSEQUENCE
Lonely

EMOTION
Shame

FROM
ISOLATION
TO
CONNECTION

DAY
68

VULNERABLE AND TRANSPARENT

HOW WELL DO YOUR PEOPLE KNOW YOU? YOU MIGHT HAVE A VERSION of your life that you share on social media, and a version you share over coffee, but does anyone know the real you?

Who knows that you lost your mind on your kids last week?

Who knows you haven't talked to your dad in a year because of hurt?

Who knows you had an abortion in college?

Who knows you are sad?

Who knows you are lonely?

In my own journey of rewiring toxic thinking patterns, I am learning to recognize the difference between vulnerability and transparency. *Vulnerability* is the edited disclosure of personal feelings or parts of yourself. *Transparency* is the exposure of the unedited, unfiltered, and unflattering parts of your soul. Vulnerability is precious and useful and can serve great purposes, and it's as far as you need to go with most acquaintances (and for sure as far as you should go for Facebook). But transparency is necessary with your closest people, and especially with God. It's the only way you can truly be known. Nonetheless, it's a scary idea that can send you into spirals of isolation and hiding.

Hiding could include retreating behind things like Instagram posts, a cute outfit, obedient kids, an organized home, or a meaningful job. But no matter what we arrange on the outside, we can't hide our eyes. Do you know what I see when I look into the eyes of some of the men and women I meet, people like you who are trying to do and be their best?

I see longing.

To be seen.

To be loved.

To be right with people and God.

To be whole.

We all wish we didn't need things outside ourselves. We try to prove we don't need anyone. We take pride in going it alone, in making it through a rough week without seeking help. We may barely realize it, but we all are hanging on to self-sufficiency.

Yet to love is to be vulnerable and transparent. Just as God created us to need water and food every few hours, He created us to need relationships. Our needs eventually bring us out of hiding. But whatever we choose to nourish ourselves with will determine whether we return to hiding or instead discover how to enjoy our lives again, to enjoy people and relationship again, and to enjoy Him again.

Enjoying anything will be difficult if you're constantly giving in to the spiraling thoughts that cause you to withdraw from others— thoughts that keep you focused on the hurt, regret, burnout, demands, or conflict you might be facing. But an encounter with Jesus is enough to change all that. Jesus will meet and feed you when you risk vulnerability and transparency and choose to connect—first with Him, then with others.

MEDITATE:
Jesus said to them, "I am the bread of life; whoever comes to me shall not hunger, and whoever believes in me shall never thirst." (John 6:35)

REWIRE THE SPIRAL:
I choose to risk being known.

Jesus, You gave me my longing to be seen and loved. Help me choose You first, so I can be healthy and free with the people in my life. Amen.

DAY
69

SEEN AND LOVED

HUMAN BEINGS NEED TO BE *SEEN* AND *LOVED* TO TRULY THRIVE. DO YOU know what it is to feel that way? Feeling seen and loved is the foundation and framework from which we build and grow. When we lack connection and relationship, everything around us seems to crumble into pointlessness and despair. As counselor and author Larry Crabb wrote, "No lie is more often believed than the lie that we can know God without someone else knowing us."[1]

We were created to be seen and loved. And we were built to be known by other people.

We can't curl up on our couches, read a book, pray, and simply *will* our minds to change all by themselves. For lasting transformation, we need the Holy Spirit, and we need other human beings. God is concerned not only with the posture of our hearts but also with the people on our arms. In terms of fulfilling our mission in this life, we can't do anything worthwhile alone. So He places us in community.

---

1   Larry Crabb, *SoulTalk: The Language God Longs for Us to Speak* (Brentwood, TN: Integrity, 2003), 138.

In fact, God Himself exists in community—the Trinity relating as Father, Son, and Holy Spirit. Three persons, one God. Perfect community. If God Himself lives in community, I would say we need it too.

And if His example isn't clear enough, we have countless verses in the Bible that speak to the necessity of community, most notably these from Paul: "Live in harmony with one another."[2] "Comfort one another, agree with one another, live in peace."[3] "Do not use your freedom as an opportunity for the flesh, but through love serve one another."[4] "Be kind to one another, tenderhearted, forgiving one another."[5] If you notice, Paul assumes we're already living in a tight community, and he offers these statements as encouragement in *how* we ought to live in community. Unfortunately, the idea of living in community is one more instruction we tend to regard as a suggestion. We'd like to do it, but when things get tough, we push it aside.

It seems that our generation has made an idol out of the very thing God is calling us away from: independence. Yet community is an essential for our lives.

What would happen if we viewed ourselves less as independent superheroes and more as village people, those who are known, noticed, loved, and seen by those around us? What would happen, today, if you chose to connect with community—even in small ways—instead of going it alone?

---

2   Romans 12:16.
3   2 Corinthians 13:11.
4   Galatians 5:13.
5   Ephesians 4:32.

MEDITATE:
Love one another with brotherly affection. Outdo one another in showing honor. **(Romans 12:10)**

REWIRE THE SPIRAL:
I was created to be seen and loved.

God, thank You for wiring me to be seen and loved, by You and by others. When I am tempted to muscle through today alone, open my eyes and heart to those around me. I want to make them feel seen and loved too. Amen.

LIFTED UP

RIGHT NOW, YOU HAVE THE POWER OF INTERRUPTION. YOU ARE NOT A victim to your mind. You can redirect your thoughts. You can change your mindset. But one of the most powerful ways you can redirect your thoughts is to allow somebody to interrupt them for you.

Recently I was so discouraged about a project I was working on that I started spiraling out. So I made a choice. I called my friend Carly.

I remember thinking, *Is this too vulnerable? Am I burdening her with my junk? Is it selfish to assume she has time to deal with all this right now?* But I went ahead and did it. I told her everything I was feeling. I told her my thoughts—even the really ugly, embarrassing ones that had me ready to quit.

And then at the end, she did an incredible thing. She started fighting for me, encouraging me, and speaking truth over me. She told me from her heart that what I was doing that day would be helpful not only for her but for others. After a few minutes, I was weeping. I thanked her for speaking life and truth over me.

It's hard to imagine what could have happened if I hadn't called her. I might have sat in toxic thoughts for days. The spiral would have continued. As it always does when left unchecked.

My story is an example of exactly why we need people to fight for us. We need people who are fierce and who are warriors and who will get their hands dirty in our defense. When we say out loud the lies that are in our heads, we need people who will fight for us with the truth.

But we also have to be those friends. And if you are wondering why you don't have those people in your life, don't be discouraged. Relationships are hard, and we usually quit them as soon as they get difficult. Yet the best ones have been through a lot of "hard." The hard times actually build the depth and maturity of a relationship. We might be able to list a lot of reasons why we don't have deep, close friendships, but we can always shift that narrative. And the best way to shift it is to be that person first.

So who can you fight for today? Who can you call, check up on, and encourage? That person might not know how to take it, and might even pull back. But that's okay. Don't stop trying. Once you go first and start to be that person for others, they start to fight for you too.

God gave us a gift in each other. Let's not miss out on it.

MEDITATE:

Two are better than one, because they have a good reward for their toil. For if they fall, one will lift up his fellow. But woe to him who is alone when he falls and has not another to lift him up! (Ecclesiastes 4:9–10)

REWIRE THE SPIRAL:

I can fight for my people and ask them to fight for me.

God, thank You that I am not alone on this earth—that You have put me and those around me intentionally together to lift each other up. Please make me fierce enough to fight for others and vulnerable enough to ask for help. Amen.

WHY WE GO IT ALONE

NO MATTER HOW CONFIDENT WE LOOK ON THE OUTSIDE, EACH OF US has a deeply embedded fear that haunts us every day of our lives: *If anyone really knew me, they'd leave me.*

I don't know exactly how this fear whispers to you, but if you're anything like countless others who deal with it, the terrorizing taunts probably sound something like this:

○ *If people knew what I've done, they'd want nothing to do with me.*

○ *If people saw who I really am, they'd run the other way.*

○ *If people knew the thoughts I am capable of thinking, they'd reject me from their lives.*

Or maybe the voice of this fear is more subtle:

○ *Why would I bother people with my problems?*

○ *I can handle this.*

○ *What good will it do if I let someone in, anyway?*

When we listen to lies about our worth, we naturally back away from other people. Sometimes our distancing behavior succeeds in pushing people away and ends up reinforcing our fear of rejection. This self-fulfilling thought pattern leads to our insecurity feeding our isolation, which in turn feeds the lie that we are worthless, unknown, and unworthy of care or attention. As a result, we feel unseen and unloved; and to protect ourselves from further rejection, we build higher walls and deflect anyone who might change our perception. And on it goes.

Gradually we embrace the lie that we must do life on our own, and that we must isolate ourselves to avoid risking exposure and rejection. And alone in the dark, the devil can tell us whatever he wants.

But what would it mean to "walk in the light" and have fellowship with one another, as the Bible says?

The truth is that you are designed in the image of a holy God, who embodies community and who invites you into His family. You are created for community. With that in mind, you should constantly battle the lie that you can solve your own problems. The truth is, God made you to live known and loved. You have a choice. You can interrupt isolating thoughts and instead choose to be known.

MEDITATE:
If we walk in the light, as he is in the light, we have fellowship with one another, and the blood of Jesus his Son cleanses us from all sin. (1 John 1:7)

REWIRE THE SPIRAL:
God made me to live known and loved.

Jesus, please free me from isolating thoughts. When I'm alone in the dark, help me choose truth and connection. Amen.

BETTER TOGETHER

CHOOSING COMMUNITY OVER ISOLATION CAN BE DOWNRIGHT SCARY.
It requires us to take a risk. But God purposefully places us in community so that those around us can help us in the battle for our thought lives. When our minds are chaotic, our thoughts are spiraling, and our emotions are running the show, our escape plan can include simply reaching out and whispering that little word: "Help."

Researcher and author Brené Brown said, "Vulnerability is the core, the heart, the center, of meaningful human experiences."[1] Or put another way: We must be known in order to be healthy. So tell me the people who know you and how deep that knowledge runs, and I will tell you how healthy you are.

Many of us are in trouble in that regard, though, because there are real, legitimate challenges to living in meaningful community. In fact, the more people I encounter, the more valid reasons I hear for why community "just isn't for me." For example, you might live in a super-small

---

1   Brené Brown, *Daring Greatly: How the Courage to Be Vulnerable Transforms the Way We Live, Love, Parent, and Lead* (New York: Avery, 2012), 12.

town, or perhaps you're a full-on introvert, who finds interacting with new people stressful and exhausting. Maybe you've suffered a painful betrayal—or more than one—and that keeps you from engaging now. You risked trusting someone with your struggle, and that decision came back to bite you. "Not doing that again," you say.

To these and a thousand other pushbacks, I have only one response: I get it! We can't control how people will respond once we've let them in. They might say something insensitive or be awful in some new and inventive way. People can be jerks and flighty, inconsiderate, self-centered, and forgetful. I know this because I am a person, and I've been all these things at some point. As, no doubt, you have been as well.

Nonetheless, relationships are worth the hard work. Certainly every valuable relationship in my life is one I have had to fight for.

So instead of letting the enemy hold you captive in isolation, remind yourself of this truth: *I have a choice. I can remember that the Spirit of God lives inside me and will walk with me as I reach out to others who are just as human and just as in need of connection and grace as I am.*

MEDITATE:
Be kind to one another, tender-hearted, forgiving one another, as God in Christ forgave you.
(Ephesians 4:32)

REWIRE THE SPIRAL:
People aren't perfect, and neither am I, but I can choose connection.

God, help me risk being known by You and others today. Amen.

BOTHER AND BE BOTHERED

AS WE MAKE THE CHOICE TO STOP TRYING TO DO LIFE ON OUR OWN and instead risk connection with other real-live human beings, we must have two resources at our disposal: the awareness to know what we need and the courageous gumption to go out and get it.

One of the things that takes the most gumption, though, is to bother others, and let others bother you.

As acquaintances deepen and broaden into friendships, stakes get higher. Fear of rejection is a real thing. My counsel: Go for broke. When you notice your friends aren't being themselves, bug them until they shoot straight. Invite them to tea. Invite them to lunch. Tell them you want to pray for them, because you know something is drastically wrong. Bother them until they feel safe enough to vent. They'll thank you for that bothering someday.

Likewise, to experience true community, you've got to be botherable yourself. Take the risk to trust someone with the truth of your life today. Yes, you might get hurt. Yes, you might feel embarrassed. Yes, it might be uncomfortable. But better the discomfort of a friend holding your hand and listening than the discomfort of thinking you're alone.

Notice, though, that *bother* comes before *be bothered*. This is the wisdom in Jesus's golden rule: Do unto others as you'd have them do unto you, based on Luke 6:31. So first, take the initiative. And then let others take the initiative with you.

I can't help but notice that every time I post on Instagram about friendship and the value of doing life in community, I get responses such as these:

"No one wants to be my friend."

"No one ever reaches out."

"I do my part, but no one ever reciprocates."

"Nobody cares about me."

Listen—giving thoughts such as these space in your mind and heart is giving the enemy a free pass. The irony here is that many of the people you think don't care about you are feeling the very same way. Maybe they are worried that if they put themselves out there, they will be rejected. They might be frustrated that nobody seems to be reciprocating the care they extend. They are sure no one wants to be friends with them. We're all in the same boat here.

Which is why I'm begging you: Go be the botherer first. Reach out. Take the risk. Say what you're feeling. Listen well. Be the friend you wish others would be for you.

MEDITATE:
Whatever you wish that others would do to you, do also to them. (Matthew 7:12)

REWIRE THE SPIRAL:
I can be bold and brave enough to be the botherer first.

God, please break down any walls I've built that are preventing me from experiencing deep relationship. Fill me with Your Spirit as I choose gumption and make the choice to bother and be bothered by those You've put in my life. Amen.

THE LAST 2 PERCENT

IF WE WANT TO BE FREE OF THE CHAOS, WE CANNOT STAY ALONE IN the dark with the devil. We have a choice. We can be known. We need to be rescuers, and we need to gather a team around us.

Because beautiful things happen when we let one another in.

We have this saying at my home church in Dallas: "Say the last two percent." Maybe you think you have learned the secret of mastering authenticity. You'll mention your struggle with a sin or a fear or an insecurity, but even those of us who value authenticity often have one card that we don't put down. It's the little secret we won't show our families. It's the one we won't share with our friends. Maybe your 2 percent is that you felt rage at your young children today. Or maybe it's a mistake you made years ago that you never told anyone about.

For a friend of mine—an awesome, godly woman—this was hard to do. But she mustered the courage and told one of our mutual friends that she had been attracted to a man who was not her husband, and had even started texting him. She pulled our friend aside and said, "I need to lay down the last two percent I am not sharing with anyone. I need to say it." Then she said it out loud. And here's where it gets crazy. She told me, "The moment I said it out loud, I have never been attracted to him since."

Yeah, it's crazy. Why would that happen? Let me tell you again: If you stay in the dark with the devil, he can tell you whatever he wants.

Maybe you have stayed in the dark with the devil and have kept your secrets close. Maybe you've held back from showing anyone all your cards. I mean, why would you? Maybe you think it isn't that big of a deal and doesn't mean anything. But when you don't play your last cards, the devil has you right where he wants you and can tell you whatever he wants.

The good news is, when you say out loud what's in your thoughts, and when you reveal your dark struggles, you take them captive and break their power. You test the gospel and allow it to stand. You bring in community. Because this is how God created you to fight: Known. Seen. Loved. Choose it today.

MEDITATE:
Confess your sins to one another and pray for one another, that you may be healed. The prayer of a righteous person has great power as it is working. (James 5:16)

REWIRE THE SPIRAL:
I will risk being vulnerable.

Lord, please show me where I've been holding back from those You've placed in my life to support me in pursuing You. Help me lay down my last 2 percent and choose the freedom of being known. Amen.

CALLED OUT OF HIDING

A SURPRISING THING HAPPENED AFTER A RECENT TRIP WITH GOOD friends. During the trip, we connected so well, and the time together nourished and revived my spirit. But once I returned home after experiencing such healing connection with the community I so desperately needed, I woke up lonely. It wasn't because I missed my people. It was because I had accidentally been thinking that the perfect getaway with them was supposed to fill my soul.

It's not that the trip was a letdown. On the contrary, it was amazing. It was all the things I hoped it would be. But it still did not fill my soul. I got thirsty for community again.

Here's what I believe causes situations like mine: We are so lonely and do not feel known or understood. We do not feel connected to people in a really deep way, because we are expecting them to fill a void in us only God can fill.

The lie is that good things like community, authenticity, and confession can take the place of connecting with Jesus. But in truth, **loneliness is meant to be an invitation to draw closer to God.** Still, at the first sign of loneliness, our tendency is to try frantically to meet that need with people, and to prove to ourselves that we are lovable and funny and worthy of attention. Unfortunately, if we connect with people and not with God, we end up asking people to be our enough. And people will always eventually disappoint us, because they were never meant to be our all in all.

Only God has the resources and ability to exhaustively meet your needs. To make you never thirsty again. Yes, you were also designed to need human relationships, but they can never be fully enjoyed if you're using them to replace the ultimate relationship. Only when you allow God to meet your deepest fundamental needs will you go from using people to meet your needs to enjoying people despite the ways they disappoint you.

Until you make that shift in your expectations, you will continually go back into spirals of isolation, because it's too painful to be known. You might give the illusion of sharing yourself—telling a little of the truth— but not enough to reveal your brokenness beneath the surface. You fall into the spiral of hiding away.

Yet Jesus calls you out of hiding.

He calls you to the living water that wells up and sets free and quenches and restores. Jesus says, *Let Me be your enough. You will be filled and you will be known and you will be free.*

MEDITATE:

Everyone who drinks of this water will be thirsty again, but whoever drinks of the water that I will give him will never be thirsty again. The water that I will give him will become in him a spring of water welling up to eternal life. (John 4:13–14)

REWIRE THE SPIRAL:

Only God can meet my deepest needs.

Jesus, thank You for offering freedom. I choose Your enough-ness today, over both isolation and codependency. Only You can meet my needs. Amen.

MADE TO CONNECT

DO YOU REMEMBER WHAT MIRROR NEURONS DO? WHEN YOU'RE SITTING across from somebody else—a friend over coffee, let's say—your mirror neurons are all firing. Suppose your friend shares something hard with you and has a very sad face. Before you realize you're even doing it, your face mirrors your friend's. You are suddenly sharing in the sadness. That reaction comes from something in your brain that physiologically tells you to empathize with your friend.

God gifted us with this ability, because He knew we would have to do life together, and that we couldn't just live on isolated islands going through our struggles unconnected with others. He made us to be hardwired for connection.

God addressed this connection in the very first person, Adam, in the Garden of Eden. Even at the beginning, God knew, *it's not good for man to be alone.* The same is true for us today. We all need our people. Some of us may think, *Well, it's not a big deal that I'm isolated and don't have great friends. It doesn't matter so much.* But it is a big deal.

Loneliness is an epidemic in our culture today, and it causes real, measurable health problems. Loneliness has been linked to heart disease. And depression. And chronic stress. And poor sleep.[1] If the physical hardwiring isn't enough to convince you that connection matters, maybe this will: You're at the center of a war, and when you choose isolation over connection, you are allowing the enemy to win in your life.

Maybe for you, the enemy has had a lot of success in hitting you with isolation. You have been hurt by your community, by the local church, and by those who should have brought healing into your life, and now you are completely alone. Let me tell you: Fight the enemy on this. Pray about it, and bring people in. It is a process. It takes time. But it doesn't have to take as long if you go deep fast.

The Bible tells us that we have divine weapons to destroy strongholds (2 Corinthians 10:4). One of those weapons is community. It's such a powerful weapon because God is in us. In community, a supernatural occurrence that defies understanding takes place—the Spirit of God indwelling you fights for and resonates with the Spirit of God in those around you. A sense of unity and power arises when we are together. I've seen it again and again.

When we fight for each other, our lives are changed. When we are in deep, deep community together, joy and peace mark our lives. We all need this. It is not optional. It's necessary. If that realization gives you stress, remember: You're specially designed and built for relationships. You've already got everything you need to connect.

---

1   "The Science of Love: See How Social Isolation and Loneliness Can Impact Our Health," Living Love Mindfulness Medicine, February 21, 2017, https://livinglovecommunity.com/2017/02/21/science-love-see-social-isolation-loneliness-can-impact-health.

The LORD God said, "It is not good that the man should be alone." (Genesis 2:18)

God built me to need people in my life.

God, I embrace the way You made me. Help me fight against isolation and remember that connection is essential. Whenever You open a door to go deep with someone, help me choose to take it. Amen.

POURING OUT

THE GOSPELS TELL US ABOUT A WOMAN AT A WELL. SHE GOES THERE IN the heat of the day to draw water. She avoids the cool of the morning, because she doesn't want to run into anyone. She's ostracized. Isolated. She is living in adultery and doesn't want to talk to anyone about it.

But Jesus meets her there and offers her salvation. Forgiveness. Living water. She hears this, and then she does something unthinkable. She not only runs to everyone she was hiding from, but she also runs to tell them about her sin! *I think the Messiah is here, and He knew my sin.* She *leads* with everything she has always tried to hide.

Is she crazy? Or is she changed? Free?

Perhaps the reason we isolate is because we don't know what it feels like to live wholly forgiven. We've never known what it means to truly enjoy our lives, to run into a crowd with no shame, no fear, no guilt, no feeling a need to prove ourselves, and no performance. Just us accompanied by the amazing news of a Savior who happens to change lives.

Jesus arrests us with His forgiveness and His grace, and He absolutely sets us free. He does not need us to perform. He is not here for a show.

We just get to run with Him. It doesn't make sense, and it's kind of messy, but it's wild and fun and what we are meant to do when the Spirit is filling us with everything our souls have always craved.

Being known is what happens when you realize you are already known and, because of Jesus, already accepted. You don't have to keep searching for what you already have. The living water floods in when you embrace your identity as a child of God, and then it eternally quenches your soul. In fact, it wells up and pours out of you until you have nothing left to prove and nothing left to hide.

Just look at what the living water did for the woman at the well:

○ *She went from shame and hiding to being fully known and accepted.*

○ *From avoiding people to engaging with everyone around her.*

○ *From thirsting for someone or something to fill her to being completely satisfied.*

○ *From wasting her life on sin to fulfilling her God-given purposes.*

○ *From feeling embarrassed to overflowing with joy.*

Jesus has done the same for you. So pour it out!

The woman left her water jar and went away into town and said to the people, "Come, see a man who told me all that I ever did. Can this be the Christ?" (John 4:28–29)

In Jesus, I am fully known and accepted.

Jesus, thank You for my identity as Your child, forgiven and renewed. Let Your presence change me, fill me, and pour out of me onto others. I want to overflow. Amen.

WELCOME TO THE TABLE

SATAN LOVES WHEN WE'RE ALONE. IF HE CAN ISOLATE YOU, HE CAN make you believe whatever he wants. He can make you shut down and live in his lies, believing you have to hide and that you are not enough. He wants you focused on yourself, your problems, and your sin, not fighting for the glory of God or for souls. He wants you living in fear in this world rather than looking forward to an eternity that is for sure coming.

So he will distract you . . . with Netflix. *Downton Abbey,* to be exact.

You know one of the fascinating things about *Downton Abbey?* The family doesn't go downstairs very often and the servants don't go up except to serve. They certainly don't sit on the upstairs furniture. In the social hierarchy of the time, there was a dividing wall between the rich and the poor, those who were worthy and those who were not.

Our God came to take away the walls dividing family from servants. Our God says, *Guess what? You don't stay downstairs in the servants' quarters. Come upstairs and be part of My family and enjoy the riches and goodness of life I give to My children.*

This is your worth, your value, and who you are. For eternity. No circumstance, no person, no mistake, and no lie in your own head can steal it. It is true. You can believe the lies of the enemy that keep you fearful and hiding in the shadows, but it will not for one second shift what is true.

Our identity is secure. We are part of the family, but you and I too often hesitate to go upstairs and enjoy it. We stay downstairs in hiding, even though we *know* in heaven we will be with God, at His table and enjoying Him and all He has for us. But why wouldn't we go upstairs today and have a great meal and enjoy the gracious Downton lifestyle now?

You are a child of God, adopted by the King, made to be—are you ready for this?—a co-heir with Christ. Crazy, right? Whatever Jesus Christ gets in heaven is our inheritance too. Amazing. This is our identity.

Don't you know God is looking at us and saying, *You are in My family. You are My kid. Why on earth are you hiding in the basement?* **When we hide, we diminish ourselves, we diminish our worth, and we diminish our belief in God.** When we come out of hiding, when we choose connection, we can start to enjoy all God has for us in His family.

MEDITATE:
Now if we are children, then we are heirs—heirs of God and co-heirs with Christ, if indeed we share in his sufferings in order that we may also share in his glory. (Romans 8:17, NIV)

REWIRE THE SPIRAL:
I am a child of God and a co-heir with Christ.

Father, thank You for my inheritance as Your child, and for Your promise that I don't have to hide alone. Please knit me into Your family and feed us all on Your truth. Amen.

EMOTION
Stress

THOUGHT
I can do whatever I want

BEHAVIOR
Pursues self-
indulgent comforts

RELATIONSHIPS
Self-serving

CONSEQUENCE
Bored

CONSEQUENCE
Effective

RELATIONSHIPS
Giving and loving

BEHAVIOR
Pursues the good of others

THOUGHT
God has set me free to seek the
good of others over my own comfort

**I choose to seek the good of
others over my own comfort**

EMOTION
Stress

FROM
COMPLACENCY
TO
SERVICE

THE ALLURE OF COMPLACENCY

OUR CULTURE'S IDEA ABOUT FREEDOM IS OFTEN THAT WE ARE SET FREE to do whatever we want. The irony is that when we go through seasons of doing whatever we want, those turn out to be our least content seasons. **We were not built to live for ourselves.** You and I were made to be part of an eternal story where we are fueled by our purpose: service to an unmatched God. Complacency rewrites that script entirely.

Complacency is finding comfort in mediocrity, in accepting things as they are, and in clinging to the status quo. It's behind our tendency to check out, to zone out, and to numb ourselves. After all, if our highest aim in life is simply not rocking the boat, then why *not* eat the whole pizza, drink the whole bottle of wine, finish off the half-gallon tub of ice cream, play Candy Crush for three hours straight, or stay in bed all day?

When we live by a rule of complacency, the questions driving our thought patterns are no longer *How will God use me today?* or *How can I give Jesus to someone?* Instead, we're focused on questions like: *What do I want? What do I need? How will I get what I want and need? What do I feel like doing? What will make me happier? What will make me more comfortable? What will make me look good? What will make me sound smart? What will protect me from getting hurt or from taking all the blame?*

And the question around which all the others revolve: *What will make me feel content?* I imagine few things bring the devil greater satisfaction than our comfort-seeking ways. We present no threat to him when we're wholly preoccupied with the things of this world.

Yet as today's verse reminds us, because we have been buried in Christ and raised in faith, we have already died to the things of this world. Our real life is bound up with Christ.

When you reject passivity and lean into the needs around you, you see your mind set on the things of God. When spirals of complacency seek to take you down, you have a choice to make. You can say, "I choose to seek the good of others over my own comfort."

God is never passive. God is always working for our good and His glory. The lie we have to fight is this: *I can do whatever I want.* The truth is, *God has set me free to serve others, not indulge myself.*

MEDITATE:
We were buried therefore with him by baptism into death, in order that, just as Christ was raised from the dead by the glory of the Father, we too might walk in newness of life. (Romans 6:4)

REWIRE THE SPIRAL:
I was set free to free others.

God, thank You for placing a hunger within me to see Your good work done on this earth. Please open my eyes to where complacency might be stealing my energy and help me choose something else. Amen.

MADE TO SERVE

IN THE GOSPELS, JESUS TOLD A PARABLE ABOUT SERVANTS WHO BURNED the midnight oil in their lamps, waiting for their master to come home. He was telling His disciples—and, by extension, us—*Stay dressed for action! Keep your lamps burning! Be found waiting for your master's return!*

He went on to say, "*Blessed are those servants* whom the master finds awake when he comes. Truly, I say to you, he [the master] will dress himself for service and have them [the servants] recline at table, and he will come and serve them" (Luke 12:37, emphasis added). This is what Jesus means when He says, "It is more blessed to give than to receive" (Acts 20:35).

When we are faithful to watch for opportunities to serve, when we live our lives *at the ready* for the Master's call, we're the ones who get served in the end. Our Master will actually put on an apron and tend to *our* every need.

So what is in store for the person who serves consistently?

A key reason for the lover of God to choose service over complacency is that God highly values work. He *loves* work. God clearly delighted in His creative efforts. His hard work was fueled by sheer delight.

We, too, are made to delight in our work.

It may feel satisfying to binge on snacks while scrolling social media feeds for an hour or two (or three?), but at *some* point, don't you become antsy and itchy? Doesn't your soul start screaming for something more?

Our souls are saying, "This just isn't cutting it for me!"

Our brains are hardwired to thrive when we are serving others. Research has proven that our brains actually do much better when we're on the giving end rather than the receiving end. Serving reduces stress.[1] People who live with purpose sleep better and live longer.[2] Serving others lights up a region of the brain that is part of its reward system.[3]

You and I were custom designed to play a role in God's eternal story and to experience deep and meaningful purpose, not to waste our time with snacks and flicks. We want more than that, and there's a reason we do. God made us to crave so much more. As we wait for Him actively, with lamps burning, we find it's truly more blessed to give.

MEDITATE:
Stay dressed for action and keep your lamps burning, and be like men who are waiting for their master to come home from the wedding feast, so that they may open the door to him at once when he comes and knocks.
(Luke 12:35–36)

REWIRE THE SPIRAL:
When I serve, I come alive.

God, thank You for making me to help and wiring me to love it. Show me today how I can prime myself for action and break the spiral of complacent thoughts. Amen.

1   Christopher Bergland, "3 Specific Ways That Helping Others Benefits Your Brain," *Psychology Today,* February 21, 2016, www.psychologytoday.com/us/blog/the-athletes-way/201602/3-specific-ways-helping-others-benefits-your-brain.

2   Janice Wood, "Having a Purpose in Life Linked to Better Sleep," Psych Central, August 8, 2018, https://psychcentral.com/news/2017/07/09/having-a-purpose-in-life-linked-to-better-sleep/122940.html.

3   Bergland, "3 Specific Ways."

GOD'S WILL FOR YOUR LIFE

DO YOU WANT TO KNOW GOD'S WILL FOR YOUR LIFE? I'LL GIVE IT TO you in three words:

Surrender.

And obey.

That's it! So many books have been written on finding God's will, yet—*boom*—here it is in plain sight, in Jesus's instruction to us to take up our crosses and follow Him (Luke 9:23). We think that freedom means going our own way. In fact, freedom is found in *laying our lives down* in the service of God, the One who made us, who knows us, and who has welcomed us into fellowship with Him. It is in this state of full surrender that the longing to obey rises up in us.

To live an abundant life, we must surrender and obey. We go where God says to go. We stay when God says to stay. We lean in when God whispers our name. We simply serve when He asks us to serve.

We tend to glamorize Jesus's earthly ministry, as though every moment of His existence here was star-studded with excitement and stimulation. Yes, there were definitely noteworthy occasions throughout those three years, to say the least. But apart from the miracles Jesus performed, much of His time was spent sitting across from one or two or three individuals in a small room over a simple meal, talking about forgiveness and about grace. Surrendering and obeying. Nothing flashy. Nothing "like"-able. Nothing that would lead the evening news. Just basic acts of service from one who was constantly bending down to meet the needs of people.

So we wipe down breakfast tables and speak kindly of someone who's being criticized and write thank-you notes and build spreadsheets and take a stand against injustices. We hug and teach and work. We do all these things and a bajillion more—all because God prompted us to.

And as we do these things for the glory of God, we don't have quite as much time for ourselves.

It's the joy of self-forgetfulness. It's the race we were meant to run. **We interrupt the spiral of self and the pattern of complacency when we run the race before us.**

The devil delights in distracting you because he knows that living out your purpose here is a direct result of your love for God, your wholehearted focus on Him. When you look at Jesus, you should be so moved by His love, by His grace, and by what He did for us that you can't contain yourself. So you go give Him away. It's how we're supposed to live.

God's will for your life is to live in the beautiful balance of surrender and obedience, running your race with joy.

MEDITATE:
He said to them all: "Whoever wants to be my disciple must deny themselves and take up their cross daily and follow me." (Luke 9:23, NIV)

REWIRE THE SPIRAL:
I can run my race fixed on Jesus, because God has given me everything I need.

God, I choose to take up my cross and follow You today for the joy of it. Show me what it is to find the sweet spot of obedience and surrender as I do what You've set before me. Amen.

SINGLE-MINDED SERVICE

HEBREWS INSTRUCTS US TO "THROW OFF EVERYTHING THAT HINDERS and the sin that so easily entangles. And let us run with perseverance the race marked out for us, fixing our eyes on Jesus, the pioneer and perfecter of faith" (12:1–2, NIV). I used to think that the three key elements in that passage were a linear progression. I thought I needed (first) to throw off my sin streaks—my negative thinking patterns, my hurtful attitudes, and my terribly selfish ways—so that I could (second) run my race, and then I would (third) finally see Jesus, who would be proud that I'd done the first two things.

But that's not at all how Jesus works. It is not that we need to get rid of our sin so we can run our races and see Jesus, but rather that we need to fix our eyes on Jesus so, by His example, we can be motivated to run our races and cooperate in this mission and care about the people He died to save. As we do so, the things that once entangled us tend to utterly fall away.

Do you see what a radical shift this is? As we run—as we serve others—our sin and distraction and hindrances fall off us, which only makes it easier to keep our eyes fixed on Christ.

Our singular thought—*I choose to serve*—leads to our taking risks on Jesus's behalf, which leads to our taking our eyes off ourselves and to seeing the needs of others for a change, which leads to our taking action, which leads to our depending more and more on His strength, which leads to a deeper longing to worship Him. That prompts us to long for even greater spiritual adventures, which leads us to take yet another risk. That risk would lead to more service, dependency, and so on.

Now, *that's* a spiral I can get behind.

But it won't start until we choose to run. Until we choose to serve. Until we choose to stop prioritizing personal comfort and instead help meet others' needs.

Friend, you and I need to be people who single-mindedly reject complacency and want God more than anything else on earth. Such surrender frees us from any worry about making mistakes or failing to look like those around us.

Maybe you've heard and believed the lies that you are too much, or inadequate, and it feels better to just give up and live a complacent life. But who are we to judge whether our contribution is meaningful? What if we started saying, "I'm going to do whatever You say today, God! Anything. I'm in." And if every one of us did so, I'm convinced we would be blown away by the things that would start happening in our lives and in this world.

Let us throw off everything that hinders and the sin that so easily entangles. And let us run with perseverance the race marked out for us, fixing our eyes on Jesus, the pioneer and perfecter of faith. **(Hebrews 12:1–2, NIV)**

I can run my race and throw off anything limiting the work of God in my life.

God, please bring me into Your spiral—of worship, risk, service, and dependency on You. As I choose Your way, lift me out of complacency and into Your purpose. Amen.

THE JOY BEFORE JESUS

JESUS CAME IN HUMAN FORM, AND HE SET HIS EYES ON A JOY BEFORE Him, the joy of being with us forever, reconciling men to Himself. He knew the cross was the path to joy, and He knew His life existed to save mankind. He had a big mission: to save the world.

Emptying Himself was part of that mission. Being holy and perfect was part of that mission. Taking on the likeness of man was in that mission. He did all this to reveal God to us and to reveal the way that we would be saved. He didn't empty Himself just on the cross; His whole life also said, "This is how you're going to live!"

So often we go to Jesus and make Him the Savior of our souls, but we don't look to Him as the model for how to live. So what does it look like to live with this mindset, to be single-minded, to have one focus, to have the same heart, and to do life well?

You become a servant. You consider others' interests above yours. Whatever God says to do, you do.

Scripture is clear that Jesus "came not to be served but to serve, and to give his life as a ransom for many" (Mark 10:45). And there is no greater demonstration of this truth than Jesus humbling Himself, leaving heaven to come to earth in the form of a vulnerable baby, suffering unjust accusations, and enduring death on a Roman cross.

The race that was set before Jesus involved emptying Himself, taking on the past and present and future sin of all humankind, and spending three days in a tomb.

And yet. He did all these things, never once losing touch with joy.

Jesus knew that His race centered on a mission that was big.

He knew His race would take Him right to the cross.

But here is something else He knew: Fulfilling the mission God had asked Him to fulfill was the best possible use of His life.

"For the joy set before him." That joy is real, and it is coming for us too. We have a future and a hope. We are set free to serve so our lives will point all people to the joy we have now and the joy that is to come.

I can't think of a better way to live.

MEDITATE:

For the joy set before him he endured the cross, scorning its shame, and sat down at the right hand of the throne of God. Consider him who endured such opposition from sinners, so that you will not grow weary and lose heart. (Hebrews 12:2–3, NIV)

REWIRE THE SPIRAL:

My mission is to serve like Jesus.

Jesus, thank You for the joy set before me. Thank You for the sacrifice You made. I pray You would use my life as I choose to serve mankind the way You did—with single-minded joy in the Father. Amen.

DAY

84

GET ON THE FIELD

TRY THIS: TAKE A QUICK INVENTORY OF YOUR THOUGHT LIFE. HOW many of your thoughts in the last twenty minutes were about yourself in some form or fashion? About your feelings, frustrations, worries, or doubts? Maybe you were thinking about how to help children in Ethiopia. If that's you, I love that about you. Keep on doing that. If you *were* thinking about yourself, stay with me.

Self-focused thoughts are a breeding ground for spirals of all kinds, and they lull us into self-soothing and complacency. We get involved in making ourselves comfier, so much so that we miss our lives and instead sit in recliners on the sidelines. I'm telling you, the antidote for complacency and the weapon against it is service. It is getting in the game and refusing to sit on the sidelines. It's serving God.

Perhaps you feel like stepping back and taking a seat because you don't know exactly what to do to serve. It overwhelms you. You wonder, *What does it look like to use my gifts to help people? I don't know what I'm good at. I don't know what God wants me to do.* You know what? There is need right in front of you. You don't have to go find some mysterious calling or a mission field. God has called you to a mission field right where you are. What is the need in your neighborhood? What is the need in your kids? What is the need in your kids' friends' lives? In your marriage? In your friends' lives? Look right in front of you and meet the need. As you do it, you may feel a stretch. For some of us, service goes against our instinct. Most of us don't wake up in the morning thinking, *How can I help people today?* But those who do, know that it's delightful to help people. It's a great way to live.

The supernatural power of service is that you are not so focused and fixated on yourself. When you shift your gaze, you will be able to see that there's a greater plan for your life than building one of comfort. You can interrupt the spiral of self and the pattern of complacency when you re-direct both your thoughts and your actions toward others. When you get up, wake up, and jump onto the field—whatever field is in front of you.

So consider, what could happen if you entered the field in your life today?

MEDITATE:
Whatever your hand finds to do, do it with your might.
(Ecclesiastes 9:10)

REWIRE THE SPIRAL:
The perfect opportunity to serve is right in front of me.

God, by Your Spirit, lead me to the work You have for me, right in front of my nose. I trust that You can use my actions for good as I stand up and choose to love others in the place where You've set me. Amen.

GIVE HIM AWAY

I FEAR WE HAVE GLAMORIZED WHAT IT MEANS TO FOLLOW JESUS. WE think it happens on stages and in books and on podcasts, but it happens around tables, in neighborhoods, and in living rooms. In fact, I bet the top five people who have changed your life were eye to eye across from you, investing time in your life.

The world around us is hungry and thirsty, full of people who long for their lives to mean something. Your neighbors might be going through divorces, the death of children, or abuse, and they may be praying at night that there is a God. You can take Him to them. Do not miss out on the joy of getting to give away God to people. It is what we were built for. We can use our gifts, somehow, some way, anywhere, any time. Forget about the size or the numbers in your church or your reach on social media. Forget about how you might come off, or whether you're able to make it look good. Sharing God doesn't have to be perfect and can be messy, as long as God's there.

We have a lot of excuses about why He could never move through us, and we let that keep us complacent. These are still the lies I fight: *I am not enough. I don't have enough. There is not enough.*

But then I think about being part of this epic story of God, and the gift of being able to help bring His freedom to the people on earth. Can you imagine?

He is waiting. He wants to go crazy through you. You don't feel like you measure up? You are exactly who God is looking for. You are the one He is after. He wants you and me: the losers, the broken, the sinful, the ones who know and accept how great is our need of Him. That is how He works. Every single person in the Bible, besides Jesus, was broken, afraid, insecure, fearful, busy, and did not have enough time or money or energy or enough of anything—yet God moved through them to change history.

You might wonder how God could change history through you. You might feel broken, afraid, insecure, fearful, busy, and inadequate yourself, but remember that our weakness has never been a problem for God. And sometimes even the smallest moments are the ones God uses to change lives. It might look like you inviting a neighbor for coffee or sending a handwritten note of encouragement to a co-worker. It might mean paying for a stranger's lunch or giving up your Netflix time so you can play a board game with your kids. It might even be sitting with one person, opening the Bible, and saying, "Do you know Jesus?" That is a small step that makes a big impact.

In these and other small ways, eternity is shifted through the power of Jesus working through you. And the only way you can enjoy the work and joy He has for you here is to do life with Him and for Him.

He saved us, not because of works done by us in righteousness, but according to his own mercy, by the washing of regeneration and renewal of the Holy Spirit. (Titus 3:5)

REWIRE THE SPIRAL:

I can share God exactly where I am today.

God, thank You for using me, renewing me, and filling me enough to the point that I can give You away. Because You are enough, help me resolve to not let anything hold me back today. Amen.

TAKE A RISK

COMPLACENCY IS A SPIRAL THAT MIGHT NOT SEEM LIKE A SPIRAL. IN-stead, it seems safe. And we all want to feel safe, right? Why risk our comfort for the unknown? Because on the other side of God-oriented, Scripture-informed risk is everything we are looking for: nearness to Jesus, greater faith in His power, deeper and richer experiences and rela-tionships, and satisfaction and enjoyment in the short life we have been given.

Our hearts naturally move to self-protection and away from risk. Al-though deep in our souls we crave adventure, somewhere along the way, many of us have stifled that craving, preferring known expectations and controlled, predictable outcomes. We've lost our capacity to risk, to ex-plore, to invent, to create, and to press into scary new experiences, and instead we've created safe lives where our biggest goal is to measure up and be accepted and be enough.

But Jesus lives on the other side of our comfort zones. When we get comfortable for too long, we start to miss our need for God. With that in mind, I think there should be a God-honoring, obedient risk in our lives every single day. And as we step out of the boxes we have built and begin to serve, our hearts wake up. The Spirit of God stirs us toward a wild, uncontrolled adventure, even if it plays out in the "mundane" parts of our lives.

Every time we risk, we place our lives into the hands of our God and test His enoughness. It is for our freedom and joy that we stand out past the limits and confines of our comfort. To experience God's enoughness, we must willingly take risks for the glory of God.

I love that Jesus teaches us about where our abundance will come from before He calls us to risk. It will not be through our power and striving that anything will happen. Obedient risk will simply be us leaning into His abundance, leaning into His love, believing that He will work, and believing that He will take any situation and any boring day and cause life change to happen in it.

This is the way the Spirit moves.

Is there a risk He is calling you to? Is there someone outside your circle to befriend? Is there a person you need to tell about Christ? Is there someone to forgive? Is there a need you are supposed to meet? Choose to take a risk and do it, knowing there is no safer risk than throwing the purpose of your life on an eternal, loving, steadfast God.

Not that we are sufficient in ourselves to claim anything as coming from us, but our sufficiency is from God.
(2 Corinthians 3:5)

REWIRE THE SPIRAL:
I can risk serving the people God has put in my life, because He is worth it.

Jesus, when the patterns of my mind pull me toward complacency, fill me with that sense of adventure that leads me to risk my comfort for Your true joy. You are more than sufficient. Amen.

LOVING OTHERS FEEDS THE SPIRIT

AREN'T YOU GRATEFUL FOR THINGS THAT PULL US OUT OF COMPLA-cency? I think about how many times I have been forced to get up off my rear because of something on my plate. On so many days, I'd love to shut myself in and watch three seasons of something soothing on TV, but the truth is, I have a deadline. Or somebody who needs me. Or a meeting to serve an organization I care about.

We should recognize the blessing of having things to propel us out of bed and away from our screens on any given day. Because something happens when we take too long of a break: We start to spiral. When I don't have enough to do, I get selfish, I get complacent, and I get lazy and materialistic. I feed my flesh, and my flesh grows. But conversely, when I feed the spirit, the spirit grows—and service feeds the spirit. Sacrifice feeds the spirit. That's a choice we can make every day.

Now, I'm not talking about choosing sacrifice for the sake of sacri-fice. Or about avoiding breaks or depriving ourselves of rest. I'm talking about obedient, godly, risky sacrifice and service for the glory of God. And yes, it is a more difficult way to live. It goes against our flesh and what we want to do with our own freedom. But I'm telling you, it is how we were created to live. We are not joyful or free any other way.

Do you want your mind to be free? Embrace what pulls you out of yourself. Go serve people. Eventually, you'll get out from under the idolatry of yourself, and your mind will start to change.

When we notice our thoughts, that perhaps we're starting to numb out or spiral around and around our own selves and our own comforts, we have the freedom to do something about it. We don't have to be ashamed or push it under the rug. We're not helpless against this stuff. We can take the power of choice God has given us, quit being so selfish and complacent, and go change the world. That's what God wants for us. He has a plan for us to shift our circumstances and our minds so we can shift our world. And as we make small choices to serve others, the world changes a little bit by a little bit.

Don't worry if you don't feel up for it. The Holy Spirit is in you. God loves you, is fighting for you, and is with you. As you start to get out of your head and into service, He'll help you take greater strides for His kingdom and for His glory.

MEDITATE:
Whoever refreshes others will be refreshed. (Proverbs 11:25, NIV)

REWIRE THE SPIRAL:
My small choices to serve bring joy and connection.

God, I want to take Your hand and be pulled out of complacency today. Help me stay close to You and be guided to change the world in Your strength with my choices. Amen.

THE VINE

TODAY I WANT TO LAUNCH YOU INTO THE WORLD WITH A CRYSTAL-clear vision of how we can live out the awesome calling of God for our lives. John 15 lays this out so beautifully, and I want you to hear Jesus's words from that chapter in a new way. This is how I see His heart and vision for you through those words to His disciples, and what He would say to us:

My child, there is so much I have taught you, so much I have shown you, but I want to make plain the most urgent thing. I want you to understand what it means to do this life without Me here beside you. Trust Me, it is better if I go away. I will send a Helper who will fill you, equip you, remind you of truth, and stick with you.

This relationship with Me is just beginning. Let Me tell you how to enjoy it as your lives unfold. Because here, in this world, you will have trouble. But take heart: I have overcome the world.

Do you remember when we walked through the vineyards together? We saw the vinedresser pruning back the branches. That is how the

Father tends to you, cutting you back. It is painful and may seem unjust at times, but He only cuts back the branches He loves. Do not fear pain; receive it and watch as it causes much more fruit to be born through you.

Do not strive to produce fruit. It is impossible. I am the vine and the source; you are simply the branches, attached to Me. As you stay near to Me, intimately close to Me, I will flood you with nourishment, with life, with peace and joy, and your little branch lives will bear an abundance of fruit. This is how it works.

If we don't stay connected, you will wither up. You will feel empty and thirsty and overwhelmed with this life and your sin. Unable to sustain yourself, you certainly won't be able to help anyone else. But if you remain in Me and near Me, I will not only give you water and life, I will build healthy, life-giving fruit through you. The overflowing wine, the spring of water welling up, the miraculous bread for the hungry, the healing and rest you long for, the power and hope over death—all this will pour into you and through you to a starving, thirsty world.

But never forget where all this and more is found.

Remember, it is only in Me, with Me, through Me, because of Me that you have life to enjoy and give away.

—Jesus

MEDITATE:

I am the vine; you are the branches. Whoever abides in me and I in him, he it is that bears much fruit, for apart from me you can do nothing. (John 15:5)

REWIRE THE SPIRAL:

When I stay close to Jesus, He will overflow through me.

Jesus, You are my vine. Help me remain grafted into You through-out every minute of this day, so You can pour into the world through me. Amen.

ENDLESS GRACE

ONCE DURING A COUNSELING SESSION, MY COUNSELOR SAID TO ME, "Jennie, you sure do say the word *should* a lot. I'd be curious how often you're saying that to yourself about your day, about the things that you're doing in your life."

My answer? *A lot.*

*I **should** be doing better by now. I **should** be capturing every thought. I **should** be making better choices and spiraling less and less. I should, should, should.*

Maybe it's time for us all to take a break from *should* and breathe in some grace. I hope you feel the grace of God today—that you rest in it, even as you recognize that you also want more and different for your life and for the health of your mind. Not because God will scold you if you don't, but because it's how you were built to live—especially as a new creation.

You are not at home in your sin. You're not at home in your stuckness. You were built to run a mission that God has prepared in advance for you. And as you do that, you get to know delight in your relationship with God as you're running with Him. Delight and grace too.

True, some days you need a boss. Some days you don't need compassion. You need somebody to grab you by the shoulders and look you in the eyes and say, "*Stop that spiral! You can do it. You can stop.*" And that's true. Scripture even talks to us that way in many cases. Thank God for that. But other days, we need kindness and compassion to lead us into a deeper relationship with God. We need someone to say, "*Yes, stop! But when you can't, when it feels like you're spiraling again on that same thing, God loves you and wants to help.*"

You aren't especially messed up because you struggle again and again. In fact, the whole Bible is about people who kept messing up. Jesus even commands us to be patient with each other and to forgive each other "seventy-seven times." That statement hints at the idea that our need for grace is endless, and that we need to be compassionate and gracious with each other—and ourselves—over and over again. One day we will be made perfect and whole, but it won't be on this earth.

So whenever you start to feel beat up and tired, don't give up on choosing what is true. Instead, find compassion and grace in others, in your relationships, and especially with God as you struggle. Because you won't always need a solution or a should. But you will always need God's grace: to breathe it in, and to give it away.

"Lord, how often will my brother sin against me, and I forgive him? As many as seven times?" Jesus said to him, "I do not say to you seven times, but seventy-seven times." (Matthew 18:21–22)

Even when I fail, God won't leave me or give up on me.

Father, wash me in Your grace. Comfort me with Your love. I'll turn to You, over and over, knowing You have endless love to give. Amen.

LIFE OUTSIDE THE SPIRAL

THINKING WITH THE MIND OF CHRIST

WHO CAN FULLY UNDERSTAND HOW WE'VE MOVED FROM BEING SLAVES of sin to being children of God? We will probably be trying to wrap our minds around this astonishing truth until we get to heaven. But we must try, because it changes our identity.

As God's children, filled with the Holy Spirit, we *have* the mind of Christ (1 Corinthians 2:16). The issue is whether we're *using* it to think the thoughts that Jesus might think. Are we taking every thought captive and training our minds daily on the right paths? Are we making choices to help shift our thinking from self-defeating and self-denigrating thoughts to the truth about God and the truth about us?

Thinking with the mind of Christ means that:

Because Jesus trusted the heavenly Father in His deepest moment of grief before He went to the cross, you can choose to stop being afraid of what the future holds and trust God. *You can choose trust over fear.*

Because Jesus stole away from the crowds to be with His Father, you can choose to be still with God instead of distracting yourself. *You can choose stillness over noise.*

Because Jesus had every reason to distrust others but loved even the tax collector and prostitute, you can choose to delight in God and the people around you. *You can choose delight over cynicism.*

Because Jesus made Himself a servant by taking on human flesh, you can choose to serve God and others over yourself. *You can choose humility over self-involvement.*

Because Jesus won the victory over sin and death, you can choose to be grateful, no matter what life brings. *You can choose gratefulness over victimhood.*

Because Jesus chose to live in community with twelve men before He ascended into heaven, you can choose to let people know you instead of isolating yourself. *You can choose connection over isolation.*

Because Jesus didn't stop at the cross but promised us the Holy Spirit as our Helper, you can choose to get out there and do something. *You can choose service over complacency.*

Because Jesus did these things, you and I can choose to do the same.

MEDITATE:
God sent forth his Son, born of woman, born under the law, to redeem those who were under the law, so that we might receive adoption as sons. . . . So you are no longer a slave, but a son, and if a son, then an heir through God. (Galatians 4:4–5, 7)

REWIRE THE SPIRAL:
I can choose the mind of Christ.

Jesus, You paved the way to freedom. Thank You for making it possible to free my mind from the spirals that pull me down, simply by choosing You. Please lead me down better paths today. Amen.

DAY

91

THE OBJECT OF OUR GAZE

IN ONE OF MY FAVORITE BIBLE STORIES, WE READ THAT JESUS "MADE the disciples get into the boat and go before him" on a lake, while He dismissed the crowds of people He had just miraculously fed (Matthew 14:22). After that, He went off to pray. Later that night, He came out to them on the boat, walking across the water, wind and waves around Him. The disciples thought He was a ghost at first, but then He said, "Take heart; it is I. Do not be afraid" (verse 27).

Peter, go-getter that he was, asked Jesus to invite him to come out on the water to Him. Jesus agreed, so Peter stepped out of the boat. "But when he saw the wind, he was afraid, and beginning to sink he cried out, 'Lord, save me.' Jesus immediately reached out his hand and took hold of him, saying to him, 'O you of little faith, why did you doubt?' And when they got into the boat, the wind ceased. And those in the boat worshiped him, saying, 'Truly you are the Son of God'" (Matthew 14:30–33).

That picture of Peter with singular focus on the face of Christ, baby-stepping over those cresting whitecaps—it's powerful. And it's us. In our lives, regardless of the wind and the rain and the uncertainty and the fear, when our eyes are fixed on Jesus, we can travel *on top of*—and not under—those waves. When we shift from the thoughts that distract and choose to fix our thoughts single-mindedly on Him, everything changes!

But it wasn't Peter's strength or willpower that kept him afloat; it was the object of his gaze: Jesus's face.

If we think on Christ, if we zoom in and are consumed with Him, then everything else grows strangely dim. But the enemy wants you to focus on anything but Jesus. Because we get really dangerous when we get single-minded. Peter did. When that happened, the church was launched into existence, thousands were saved and began to follow Jesus, countries were evangelized, and generations were changed forever.

You might be thinking, *Well, that's great for Peter. But before I can change the world, I would just like to quit feeling so anxious.* I know. But part of quitting feeling anxious is finding an altogether different reason to live. When Christ is our prize and heaven is our home, we get less anxious because we know our mission, our hope, and our God cannot be taken from us. When we focus on Him, we can step forward.

MEDITATE:
Jesus immediately reached out his hand and took hold of [Peter]. (Matthew 14:31)

REWIRE THE SPIRAL:
Focus on Jesus renews my mind.

Jesus, You are my prize. Make me single-minded today as I focus on You, stepping forward through whatever's in my path. Amen.

CONTAGIOUS MINDS

HAVE YOU EVER "CAUGHT" SOMEONE'S BAD ATTITUDE? OR HAD SOME-
one's good attitude completely change the course of your day? Have you
ever made an effort to lift the atmosphere in a room and seen others respond to it? The thing is, we all have contagious minds, and it runs in
deeper levels than we think. As we seek freedom in our thoughts, we in-
troduce others to the fact that freedom is in fact possible.

This entire journey of stopping spiraling thoughts comes down to
our thoughts being wholly consumed by the mind of Christ. This matters because our thoughts dictate our beliefs, which dictate our actions,
which form our habits, which in turn compose the sum of our lives. As
we think, so we live. When we think on Christ, we live on the foundation of Christ, with our gaze fixed immovably on Him. But it doesn't
stop with us—the goal is not just one healthy mind inside your head,
beautiful as that may be. It's a healthy mind in an ecosystem of others.

This is my prayer for all of us. If thousands of people start to choose
better, get out of their heads, and shift their spirals toward the mind of

Christ, this way of thinking can become contagious—and we could see a generation freed.

I believe it is possible. I pray it will be so.

Press on, my friend. "Do not be conformed to this world, but be transformed by the renewal of your mind, that . . . you may discern what is the will of God" (Romans 12:2). Why? Why would that matter so much—to discern the will of God? Because He isn't just after your freedom. He prepared good works in advance for you so that a whole lot of other people could be set free too (Ephesians 2:10).

When you take every thought captive and reclaim your thinking patterns from the lies of the enemy, you are set free to set others free. May you steward your freedom well.

MEDITATE:
We are his workmanship, created in Christ Jesus for good works, which God prepared beforehand, that we should walk in them. (Ephesians 2:10)

REWIRE THE SPIRAL:
My thoughts can give life to others.

God, I pray that You would set me free. In Your power, help me fight the enemy hell-bent on destroying me and help me remember that the power to choose a different way is mine in You. And then help me give that away to a world aching for a new way to live and think. In Jesus's name, amen.

IF I WERE YOUR ENEMY

IF I WERE YOUR ENEMY, THIS IS WHAT I WOULD DO: MAKE YOU BELIEVE you are helpless against your spiraling thoughts. Make you believe you are insignificant. Make you believe that God wants your good behavior more than freedom for your mind.

But now you're wise to this. You are in the Word and on your knees, choosing and fighting and looking toward Jesus and the mind of Christ. God is moving through you, and you are getting dangerous. You are free and leading other people to freedom. The old lies are no longer adequate.

So if I were your enemy, I would make you numb and distract you from God's story. I would draw your attention with technology, social media, Netflix, travel, food and wine, comfort, and noise. I would not tempt you with notably bad things, or you would get suspicious. Instead I would distract you with everyday comforts to make you forget God. Then you would start to love **distraction** and **complacency** more than peace and service and loving others.

If that didn't work, **I would attack your identity. I would make you believe you had to prove yourself.** Then you would focus on yourself instead of God. Friends would become enemies. Teammates would become competition. You would **isolate** yourself and think you are not enough. You would get depressed and be ungrateful for your story. Or you would compare and believe you are better than others. You would become **cynical** and condemn others rather than love and invite them in. Either way you would lose your joy, because your eyes would be fixed on yourself and people instead of on Jesus.

And if that didn't work, **I would intoxicate you with the mission of God rather than with God Himself.** Then you would worship a cause instead of Jesus. You would fight against others to have the most important roles. You would burn out from striving. You would think that success is measured by the results you see. Then all your time and effort would be spent on maintaining **self-importance** rather than on knowing Jesus and loving people.

And if that didn't work, **I would make you suffer.** Then maybe you would think God is evil rather than good. Your faith would shrink, and your **fear and anxiety** would grow. You would get bitter and weary and tired, spiraling into **victimhood** rather than flourishing and growing and becoming more like Christ.

The enemy is telling you that those downward spirals are just the way things are. But we have the power to shut them down through Jesus—through His power, His victory, His truth, and His mind. Remember, we have a choice to change what we set our minds on.

MEDITATE:
Be sober-minded; be watchful.
Your adversary the devil prowls
around like a roaring lion,
seeking someone to devour.
(1 Peter 5:8)

REWIRE THE SPIRAL:
I am not helpless to the enemy;
Jesus will always win.

*Jesus, give me strength today as
I say to the enemy, "No more. I
choose quiet, service, wonder,
and connection. I choose humility,
gratefulness, and trust. I choose
my Jesus." Amen.*

ENOUGH

FOR SO MANY YEARS, I'VE HAD A VOICE IN MY HEAD SAYING, *I AM NOT enough.* Is it possible you hear that same voice?

We all fight feelings of inadequacy. We walk around desperately afraid we don't measure up. We slap on self-esteem strategies that feel a little like playing pretend dress-up—*Look at me! I've got it all together! How am I doing? Fine, thanks! Not spiraling at all!* But deep in our marrow we know it is pretend. *We are not enough.* So we spend our lives trying to hustle the best we can.

But God has a different storyline for us, one in which our souls are content, our minds are at peace, and epic stories unfold through our lives here—but not because of us.

In spite of us.

What if there was a story where the ones who aren't enough, the ones who recognize they don't measure up, are the very ones the God of the universe picks to move wildly in and through?

What if I told you today you could stop trying so hard and simply rest?

What if I told you today you could start enjoying yourself and your life without performing or striving or trying to wrestle control of your thoughts for another minute?

What if I told you that you don't measure up? And that it's okay? In fact, it's necessary.

Truth is, this battle for your mind requires more than you can deliver. As do your circumstances, your challenges, and the things you and your loved ones are going through. It's all too much for us. But not too much for God. He gives us yet another choice: how we will move forward. Striving, pretending, white-knuckling—or free?

My dream is that you would embrace your worst fears head-on and find that your God is enough for them. My prayer is for you to start enjoying the freedom that comes when you quit trying to prove yourself, and when you surrender what is out of control to the One who is in control.

We strive to be seen, to be known, to matter. We're desperate to believe we are doing a good job at whatever has been entrusted to us.

But we are not enough. We are not God. We don't have all the answers, all the wisdom, all the strength, or all the energy. We are finite, sinful beings. And that is okay.

In fact, it is this confession that unleashes the freedom we are aching for: *I'm not enough. So I choose to rest in surrender to the One who is.*

MEDITATE:
He said to me, "My grace is sufficient for you, for my power is made perfect in weakness." (2 Corinthians 12:9)

REWIRE THE SPIRAL:
I don't have to be enough, because God is.

Father God, I may not be enough today, but I know that You are. Show me the balance of where I am to act, and where I am to rest in Your sufficiency, sustained by Your strength. Amen.

LIVING WATER

WE RARELY GO TO GET A DRINK UNLESS WE ARE THIRSTY. BUT WHEN we're thirsty, we know the signals. That's because God built our bodies to signal our thirst for water, and He built our souls to signal our thirst for living spiritual water. To feel our thirst for God is one of God's greatest gifts to us. To recognize our need for God is the beginning of our finding Him. As we battle for freedom in our minds, we have to stay fully hydrated on those streams of living water from God.

In today's verse from the mouth of Jesus, the original Greek phrase indicates that these streams of living water will flow "from his innermost being" or "out of his belly" or from the very depths of us. So Jesus is saying to all who are thirsty, *Come back to Me, and I will keep satisfying you. And out of that life with Me, from the deepest parts of you, love will overflow and bring life to others.*

I'm convinced that our perspectives will shift as together we witness a pattern of Jesus telling us again and again that we are not enough, but that He is more than enough. **He is enough, so we don't have to be.** In fact, it is downright arrogant to keep trying to be. The reality is that He is the enough we could never be.

Because Jesus is enough, we can experience true fulfillment.

Because Jesus is enough, we can live connected with Him and others.

Because Jesus is enough, we can rest.

Because Jesus is enough, we can risk for His glory.

Because Jesus is enough, we can trade fear for hope.

Because Jesus is enough, we can embrace grace.

Because Jesus is enough, we can live out our true calling.

You can choose to live in these overflowing streams of His enoughness. Will you choose Him instead of living pulled along into spirals, missing your life, and unable to take a deep breath? Will you let Him save you?

Jesus redeems our spirals because He promises to use our worst moments and our best moments alike for His glory and our good. Every day we still make mistakes. The fact that you are fighting sin and darkness doesn't prove you are not a Christian; if Christ were not in you, you wouldn't even care. But He is in you and with you, helping fight your sin and redeeming all of it for His purposes. He holds you up and together every day. And He satisfies the thirst of your soul. Why would you ever turn to anything else?

MEDITATE:
Let anyone who is thirsty come to me and drink. Whoever believes in me, as Scripture has said, rivers of living water will flow from within them. (John 7:37–38, NIV)

REWIRE THE SPIRAL:
Jesus is enough, so I can rest today.

God, You are my source. Keep me coming back to You for nourishment, and for the waters of life that keep me going. I want to know Your enoughness through and through. Amen.

SOUL REST

WHEN GOD PROMISES US REST, HE ALMOST ALWAYS IS TALKING ABOUT *soul rest*. It's why most of the ways we try to rest actually make our insides more chaotic. TV, sleep, Facebook surfing—all fall short because nothing but Jesus can bring rest to the chaos swirling inside us.

We fall short and fail to experience rest when we try to do the work of God without God.

So let's start doing things *with* God instead of *for* God.

Today He is saying, *Just ask Me. Are you for Me? Are you building My kingdom? Just ask. I am for you. You don't need to worry.* **Our true rest and confidence come from believing God can do anything, and then stepping back and letting Him.** Through finding our identity in Him, confidence streams into our souls and empowers us to move creatively and intentionally through this life and somehow rest and enjoy it as we go about epic, eternal, world-changing, supernatural work!

Do you know that God has never not delivered? Goodness, He is good and always gives us enough. But usually it is our day's portion, our daily bread with a little thrown on top for good measure to grow our faith. Tomorrow, the crowds will be hungry again. After all, each day brings new needs, new challenges, and new problems. But every day, like Jesus did when feeding the five thousand in the Bible, He opens warehouses of bread. There is more than enough, but God wants us to keep coming to Him for it. So we return to Him for our rest.

Are you worried you're not up for the challenges of today? That you'll run flat out of energy? We are all so afraid there won't be enough, but we have a God who has us.

I pray you would catch a glimpse of a God who adores you, who wants to be in the mess with you, who will never leave you, who is for you, who has all you need, even—no, especially—on the very worst days. I pray that you would rest and lean into Him for that rest. I pray that you wouldn't just rest in your eternal provision as a part of God's family but that you would rest in the everyday provision He is already dishing out everywhere you look.

He has you, and He has what you need for your soul today.

MEDITATE:
The LORD replied, "My Presence will go with you, and I will give you rest." (Exodus 33:14, NIV)

REWIRE THE SPIRAL:
I can trust God to be God and deliver all I need.

Jesus, show me what it is to find true soul rest in You. I choose to let go of imitation rest and to turn toward Your limitless love. Thank You for having me. Amen.

GOOD FRUIT

HAVE YOU EVER BITTEN INTO A PERFECTLY RIPE PEAR, AT THE PERFECT temperature, at the perfect time? Miraculous, I'd say. Definitely evidence there is a God. God creates the sweetest, most incredible-tasting things on earth—things like cold, perfectly ripe, juicy pears—and they are better than all the man-made processed food in the world. Real pears taste amazing, and they're for our good and show God's glory. No one named Harry or David could build these pears from scratch. Humans simply cannot create something like this.

In the same way, spiritual fruit—like eternity-impacting relationships, conversations, and actions—is not something we can "make" ourselves. Spiritual fruit will only emerge naturally as we seek God, love Him, spend time with Him, and abide in Him.

Let me tell you what we're doing instead: We are building Nutter Butters. Humans don't create fruit; but we sure know how to make Nutter Butters. And they taste good. I like them a lot. But everyone is getting sick on the "processed sugar" we're handing out in the form of self-help strategies and self-esteem boosts. God gave us a great identity in which we can find deep security and confidence, but it only comes from who He is and what He has done for us.

Let me be clear: Even as we search our hearts and minds for what's really going on with us, we really don't need to do the groundwork of securing our identity. We don't need to create a processed version of ourselves. We just need to be nourished naturally by God and bloom into His sweetness. We will live and love out of our view of God. And really, all we need to do is be with Him. Spend time in His presence. Because when we grow in our worship, we forget ourselves. Fixing our eyes on our God consumes us with Him and allows us to forget worrying about whether our identity is all sorted out.

Being with Jesus moves water and nourishment into and through us as branches. Connection to Him is how our thirsty souls are quenched and also how we receive a steady supply of the water required to produce mature, sweet-tasting fruit.

If a fruit tree doesn't receive sufficient water, the fruit it's producing will be sour or dry-tasting or will even just fall off rather than grow to maturity. An adequate amount of moisture is absolutely necessary.[1]

For your life to yield fruit, you need a constant supply of God—His wildly rushing, satisfying water contained just in who He is and poured onto you by your simply being near Him, knowing Him, and pressing up close to His Word and to His presence.

---

1   See www.quora.com/How-does-a-fruit-tree-produce-fruit.

MEDITATE:

He is like a tree planted by streams of water that yields its fruit in its season, and its leaf does not wither. (Psalm 1:3)

REWIRE THE SPIRAL:

When I stay rooted in Jesus, He grows fruit through me.

Jesus, I want to return to Your presence today and be supplied and satisfied by You. No processed imitation will do. I choose to be nourished by You. Amen.

TRAINING IN TRUTH

IT'S NOT EASY TO STOP BELIEVING LIES. WE CAN'T SIMPLY SIT BACK AND wait for our minds to heal, or for our thoughts to change. We have to train. That's how truth gains the victory in the battle for our minds.

So we stick our heads in our Bibles day in and day out. You might not be able to fully grab hold of truth on day 2, but on day 102, it will be taking hold in your heart and mind.

We wake up in the morning, and rather than getting on our phones, we get on our knees and submit our thoughts to Jesus.

We invest in healthy relationships and intentionally go to them when we start to spiral.

We choose well. Daily. Moment by moment.

We train our minds. And when a new temptation to spiral presents itself, we trust our training.

This works. In time, the truth sinks in. It did for me. For so long, in the dark, my mind used to spiral, afraid that there was no good place to land. Afraid that God was not real. Afraid that I was not safe. Afraid that I was not seen. Afraid of the days to come.

Those fears, I would learn, were frauds. I *was* seen. I *was* safe. God *was* real. The truth wins.

God remains so real today. I am at home with God again. He chose me. He chose me and set me apart. I am not alone in the dark. I am known. I am chosen. I am safe. I am God's, and He is mine. It's all true for me. And it's true for you too.

So again and again in the night, I make my choice. I choose to talk to God instead of doubt Him. I choose to be grateful for all He has done. I choose to obey Him, no matter how I feel.

This is my upward spiral into His truth. I am at peace. And I so desperately want this for you. I want you to live free and give Jesus to others.

God can make that kind of breakthrough happen anywhere and with anyone. His truth is powerful. So shame? Fear? Doubt? It no longer has power over you! It no longer has power over our generation! Let's train our minds to focus on that truth.

MEDITATE:
While bodily training is of some value, godliness is of value in every way, as it holds promise for the present life and also for the life to come. (1 Timothy 4:8)

REWIRE THE SPIRAL:
I'll trust my training, and trust in Jesus. Healing is a journey.

God, please be with me as I train in Your truth. As I return to it again and again, transform lies into truth, and bondage into freedom. I choose to trust Your power and Your promise. Amen.

REST AND RESCUE

DO YOU WANT TO KNOW WHY WE ARE SO TIRED? BECAUSE WE DON'T believe God. There is no remedy for our striving and spinning apart from finding our identity in Christ. He is our enough, and the degree to which we believe that is the degree to which we will stop striving, stop spinning, and stop trying to prove or fix ourselves.

I love this verse in Isaiah: "In returning and rest you shall be saved; in quietness and in trust shall be your strength" (30:15). It is in our letting go and in our trust that He rescues us. Yet how often are we still trying to muscle through? To rescue ourselves? Let's let Him rescue us.

In an emergency situation, guess what the person being rescued has to do? Trust the rescuer and cooperate with the process. You and I don't need to be the heroes who save the world. We don't need to be thought-life gurus who have kicked our brains into high gear. We just get to be part of the story of the greatest Hero of all time. Which is good news, because being the hero is a lot of pressure and a lot of dadgum work.

So you can rest because you know God is the one rescuing you and others around you from the chaos in our heads. If God has rescued us, who can possibly get to us or steal us from Him? If anything, we can rest in that knowledge alone!

We are not God's slaves. We are God's *kids,* the ones He sent His Son to rescue. He adores us, and He wants to move into the darkness with us. He wants to feed the hungry people who are coming over the hill. He wants to heal us whether we're coming to Him on the road or waiting by a pool to be rescued. This is our birthright as children of God and co-heirs with Christ. But as long as we are trying to round up enough of our own resources to take care of the problem, we will be tired and cranky and resentful.

The beautiful alternative is to believe that our God moves in miraculous ways. We get to sit back and pray to Him and break the bread we have been given and watch Him meet needs—in abundance. We can trust Him with our people and surrender to Him our ways and plans and glory. And we can love Him because He is awesome and be with Him because there is nowhere better on earth than to be with our good, loving Father.

We get to trade striving for rest. We get to trade anxiety for peace. We get to trade spinning for confidence—not confidence in ourselves but in the power of an all-powerful and heroic God, eager to rescue.

We began this journey in full awareness that there is an enemy trying to take us out in the battle for our minds. But we end in a different place. We don't end focused on an enemy or even focused on ourselves. We end focused on our God. Who He is frees us, who He is heals and rewires us, and who He is flows in and through us and changes everything. Through Him and Him alone, we are empowered with the choice to walk in that freedom, every day of our lives.

Thus said the Lord GOD, the Holy One of Israel, "In returning and rest you shall be saved; in quietness and in trust shall be your strength." (Isaiah 30:15)

God is my rescuer and ultimate healer.

Lord, thank You for offering me rest and rescue. Please gently show me where I'm wearing myself out and help me choose to trust Your process and power instead. Amen.

THE SPIRIT OF POWER

WE HAVE SO MANY CHOICES WE CAN MAKE WHEN CONFRONTED WITH toxic thought patterns—*different thoughts* we can choose to think, and thoughts that reflect the mind of Christ.

When our minds are consumed with anxiety and doubts and fears, we can choose instead to remember what's true about God. We can think about His nearness. We can think about His goodness. We can think about His provision. We can think about His love.

When we're tempted to use busyness to distract ourselves from our shame, we can choose instead to be still in the presence of God.

When we're tempted to think cynical thoughts—that life is worthless, that our efforts are pointless, that nothing matters in the end, or that no one can be trusted—we can choose instead to open ourselves up to the world around us, taking delight in God Himself and in all He has done for us.

When we're tempted to believe we're all alone in this world, we can choose instead this thought: *The Spirit of God lives inside me, and because of that, I'm never alone. There are people who love me, who want to be with me. I can reach out to them instead of sitting here, stuck.*

These are all choices we can make to reconfigure our thinking patterns and help us become whom we long to be. If you've made even a single choice on this journey that has knocked a toxic thought pattern off track, I want you to know that's a victory.

You may be thinking at this point, *Oh no, I'm still thinking negative thoughts.* You know what? You know what you're doing now that you didn't do before? You're *noticing* your thoughts. So now you know that you're having negative thoughts. Or that you're thinking about yourself too much. And prior to this, that wasn't your story.

We used to be just victims to our minds and victims to our thoughts. But when we start to see these negative patterns in our lives that maybe we didn't even know were there before, we can start to fight. We have weapons: service, gratitude, stillness with God, connection, trust, delight. These are the weapons God has given us to fight the enemies of our mind. And guess what? Y'all, God wins. These weapons are powerful enough to destroy strongholds and the strongest weapons of the enemy. They are powerful enough to change our minds.

So take every thought captive, because you are no longer in bondage to the enemy of your mind. You don't have to submit to the enemy of your mind anymore. As a child of God, you have power over your mind. So take that power and use it. Take that power and have authority over your thoughts. God has a plan for you to shift your circumstances and your mind so that you can shift your world.

MEDITATE:

God gave us a spirit not of fear but of power and love and self-control. (2 Timothy 1:7)

REWIRE THE SPIRAL:

God has redeemed my life, and He can renew my mind.

God, thank You for making different thoughts possible. Thank You for winning the war so I can fight this battle with confidence, power, and authority. Give me the strength to make whatever shift I can today, and every day. Amen.